DNA
Evidence

DNA
Evidence

Alan Marzilli

SERIES CONSULTING EDITOR
Alan Marzilli, M.A., J.D.

CHELSEA HOUSE
PUBLISHERS

An imprint of Infobase Publishing

DNA Evidence

Copyright © 2005 by Infobase Publishing

Chelsea House
An imprint of Infobase Publishing
132 West 31st Street
New York NY 10001

Library of Congress Cataloging-in-Publication Data

Marzilli, Alan.
    DNA evidence/Alan Marzilli.
        p. cm. — (Point/counterpoint)
    Includes bibliographical references and index.
    ISBN 0-7910-8092-7
    1. DNA fingerprinting—United States. 2. Evidence, Expert—United States.
3. Forensic genetics—United States. I. Title. II. Point-counterpoint
KF9666.5.M37 2004
345.73'067—dc22   2004010212

Chelsea House books are available at special discounts when purchased in bulk quantities for businesses, associations, institutions, or sales promotions. Please call our Special Sales Department in New York at (212) 967-8800 or (800) 322-8755.

You can find Chelsea House on the World Wide Web at
http://www.chelseahouse.com

Text and cover design by Keith Trego

Printed in the United States of America

Bang 21C 10 9 8 7 6 5 4 3 2

This book is printed on acid-free paper.

All links, web addresses, and Internet search terms were checked and verified to be correct at the time of publication. Because of the dynamic nature of the web, some addresses and links may have changed since publication and may no longer be valid.

CONTENTS

Foreword
Alan Marzilli, M.A., J.D.
Durham, North Carolina

The debates presented in POINT/COUNTERPOINT are among the most interesting and controversial in contemporary American society, but studying them is more than an academic activity. They affect every citizen; they are the issues that today's leaders debate and tomorrow's will decide. The reader may one day play a central role in resolving them.

Why study both sides of the debate? It's possible that the reader will not yet have formed any opinion at all on the subject of this volume—but this is unlikely. It is more likely that the reader will already hold an opinion, probably a strong one, and very probably one formed without full exposure to the arguments of the other side. It is rare to hear an argument presented in a balanced way, and it is easy to form an opinion on too little information; these books will help to fill in the informational gaps that can never be avoided. More important, though, is the practical function of the series: Skillful argumentation requires a thorough knowledge of *both* sides—though there are seldom only two, and only by knowing what an opponent is likely to assert can one form an articulate response.

Perhaps more important is that listening to the other side sometimes helps one to see an opponent's arguments in a more human way. For example, Sister Helen Prejean, one of the nation's most visible opponents of capital punishment, has been deeply affected by her interactions with the families of murder victims. Seeing the families' grief and pain, she understands much better why people support the death penalty, and she is able to carry out her advocacy with a greater sensitivity to the needs and beliefs of those who do not agree with her. Her relativism, in turn, lends credibility to her work. Dismissing the other side of the argument as totally without merit can be too easy—it is far more useful to understand the nature of the controversy and the reasons *why* the issue defies resolution.

The most controversial issues of all are often those that center on a constitutional right. The Bill of Rights—the first ten amendments to the U.S. Constitution—spells out some of the most fundamental rights that distinguish the governmental system of the United States from those that allow fewer (or other) freedoms. But the sparsely worded document is open to interpretation, and clauses of only a few words are often at the heart of national debates. The Bill of Rights was meant to protect individual liberties; but the needs of some individuals clash with those of society as a whole, and when this happens someone has to decide where to draw the line. Thus the Constitution becomes a battleground between the rights of individuals to do as they please and the responsibility of the government to protect its citizens. The First Amendment's guarantee of "freedom of speech," for example, leads to a number of difficult questions. Some forms of expression, such as burning an American flag, lead to public outrage—but nevertheless are said to be protected by the First Amendment. Other types of expression that most people find objectionable, such as sexually explicit material involving children, are not protected because they are considered harmful. The question is not only where to draw the line, but how to do this without infringing on the personal liberties on which the United States was built.

The Bill of Rights raises many other questions about individual rights and the societal "good." Is a prayer before a high school football game an "establishment of religion" prohibited by the First Amendment? Does the Second Amendment's promise of "the right to bear arms" include concealed handguns? Is stopping and frisking someone standing on a corner known to be frequented by drug dealers a form of "unreasonable search and seizure" in violation of the Fourth Amendment? Although the nine-member U.S. Supreme Court has the ultimate authority in interpreting the Constitution, its answers do not always satisfy the public. When a group of nine people—sometimes by a five-to-four vote—makes a decision that affects the lives of hundreds of millions, public outcry can be expected. And the composition of the Court does change over time, so even a landmark decision is not guaranteed to stand forever. The limits of constitutional protection are always in flux.

These issues make headlines, divide courts, and decide elections. They are the questions most worthy of national debate, and this series aims to cover them as thoroughly as possible. Each volume sets out some of the key arguments surrounding a particular issue, even some views that most people consider extreme or radical—but presents a balanced perspective on the issue. Excerpts from the relevant laws and judicial opinions and references to central concepts, source material, and advocacy groups help the reader to explore the issues even further and to read "the letter of the law" just as the legislatures and the courts have established it.

It may seem that some debates—such as those over capital punishment and abortion, debates with a strong moral component—will never be resolved. But American history offers numerous examples of controversies that once seemed insurmountable but now are effectively settled, even if only on the surface. Abolitionists met with widespread resistance to their efforts to end slavery, and the controversy over that issue threatened to cleave the nation in two; but today public debate over the merits of slavery would be unthinkable, though racial inequalities still plague the nation. Similarly unthinkable at one time was suffrage for women and minorities, but this is now a matter of course. Distributing information about contraception once was a crime. Societies change, and attitudes change, and new questions of social justice are raised constantly while the old ones fade into irrelevancy.

Whatever the root of the controversy, the books in POINT/ COUNTERPOINT seek to explain to the reader the origins of the debate, the current state of the law, and the arguments on both sides. The goal of the series is to inform the reader about the issues facing not only American politicians, but all of the nation's citizens, and to encourage the reader to become more actively involved in resolving these debates, as a voter, a concerned citizen, a journalist, an activist, or an elected official. Democracy is based on education, and every voice counts—so every opinion must be an informed one.

———————•————————•————————•—————————

During the past two decades, advances in technology have given police and prosecutors powerful new weapons in solving and prosecuting crimes. The most useful of these techniques is laboratory analysis of deoxyribonucleic acid (DNA), a complex molecule found in all living cells. Because everyone—other than identical twins—has unique DNA, investigators can compare evidence from the crime scene to a suspect's blood sample. The states and the federal government have compiled massive DNA databases, allowing police to search for suspects as they would by comparing fingerprints. However, unlike fingerprints, DNA also contains clues to a person's family tree and many secrets, such as whether a person will develop certain fatal diseases. As police try to collect DNA from more and more people, some people are concerned about the implications of a society in which the government knows its citizens' genetic secrets. Police have gone so far as to conduct "dragnets," collecting DNA samples from completely innocent people. This book examines the conflicts between law enforcement and civil liberties that have been generated by the awesome power of DNA testing.

Using DNA to Solve Crimes

For several years, police had been desperately trying to find the man who was raping and murdering teenage girls in the English countryside. In 1983 and 1986, young victims from neighboring small villages were found raped and strangled. Facing a dead end in their investigation, police tried something new, something that would radically change the direction of police work around the world.

Scientist Alec Jeffreys had developed a technique that allowed for the analysis of human deoxyribonucleic acid (DNA), a complex molecule found in living cells, and more importantly, one that varies from individual to individual. His method, he said, would allow police to test evidence from a crime scene, including blood and semen, and compare it to blood samples taken from potential suspects. Police brought semen collected from each of the victims to Jeffreys, along with blood taken from a young man they suspected in the case. Jeffreys told them that although the semen in each case was from the same man, he was not the man whom police suspected. The next step was a bold move that has been hailed as a blessing for law enforcement and a curse for civil liberties. The police asked all men, within certain age ranges, from three neighboring villages to provide blood samples so that they could compare the DNA of the killer to the DNA of the samples.

More than four thousand men were tested with no matches before the police got the break they needed. Someone reported hearing a baker named Ian Kelly say that he had taken the blood test for one of his coworkers, Colin Pitchfork. When police went to Pitchfork's house to get his real blood sample, he confessed to the crime, and the DNA samples confirmed his confession. In the years since, DNA has become one of the most powerful tools available to law enforcement officials, but to this day, civil libertarians question whether the methods employed by the police in the Pitchfork case are a threat to the privacy of innocent people.

The Genesis of DNA Testing Methods

As complex as the human body is, every cell is descended from a single cell, the fertilized egg. Obviously, it takes a lot of information to build an entire human, such as where to put the arms and legs, brain, and heart. It takes a lot more information to make every person different: tall or short, brown or blue eyes, dimples or not, and so on. This information is encoded in massive molecules of DNA, which are made up of billions of smaller molecules called bases. Although every person, other than identical twins, has different DNA, every person's DNA is made up of different combinations of the four bases nicknamed *A*, *T*, *G*, and *C*.

Most human cells contain chromosomes, which are made up of DNA and contain the information that makes everyone share certain characteristics but have his or her own unique

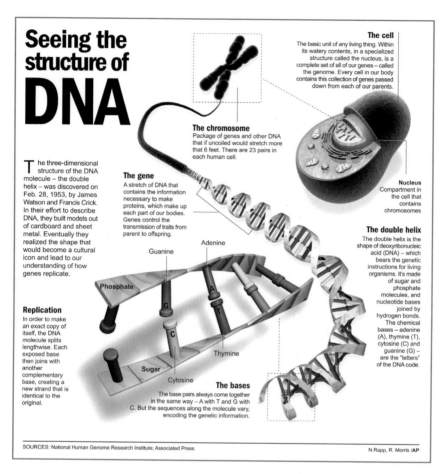

Seeing the structure of

DNA

The cell
The basic unit of any living thing. Within its watery contents, in a specialized structure called the nucleus, is a complete set of all of our genes – called the genome. Every cell in our body contains this collection of genes passed down from each of our parents.

The chromosome
Package of genes and other DNA that if uncoiled would stretch more that 6 feet. There are 23 pairs in each human cell.

T he three-dimensional structure of the DNA molecule – the double helix – was discovered on Feb. 28, 1953, by James Watson and Francis Crick. In their effort to describe DNA, they built models out of cardboard and sheet metal. Eventually they realized the shape that would become a cultural icon and lead to our understanding of how genes replicate.

The gene
A stretch of DNA that contains the information necessary to make proteins, which make up each part of our bodies. Genes control the transmission of traits from parent to offspring.

Nucleus
Compartment in the cell that contains chromosomes

The double helix
The double helix is the shape of deoxyribonucleic acid (DNA) – which bears the genetic instructions for living organisms. It's made of sugar and phosphate molecules, and nucleotide bases joined by hydrogen bonds. The chemical bases – adenine (A), thymine (T), cytosine (C) and guanine (G) – are the "letters" of the DNA code.

Adenine

Guanine

Phosphate

Replication
In order to make an exact copy of itself, the DNA molecule splits lengthwise. Each exposed base then joins with another complementary base, creating a new strand that is identical to the original.

Thymine

Sugar

Cytosine

The bases
The base pairs always come together in the same way – A with T and G with C. But the sequences along the molecule vary, encoding the genetic information.

SOURCES: National Human Genome Research Institute; Associated Press

N.Rapp, R. Morris /AP

The above diagram explains the structure of deoxyribonucleic acid (DNA), the molecule in living organisms that comprises each individual's genetic identity. Investigators are now engaged in the controversial practice of testing DNA (extracted from blood, semen, and skin) collected from crime scenes to prove a suspected criminal's guilt or innocence.

features. A gene is a stretch of DNA that has a specific function, and they come in various versions called alleles. For example, a particular allele might make a person more likely to develop breast cancer. Each person, however, also has a great deal of unique DNA that is not considered part of the genes and has no known function. Although this DNA is often called junk DNA, it does serve at least one purpose: it makes DNA testing possible because it differs so greatly from person to person.

In law enforcement, DNA testing can be used in several ways. It can be used to test crime scene evidence, such as blood, semen, or skin from underneath a victim's fingernails, to determine whose DNA is in those samples. It can be used to test weapons or clothing taken from a suspect to determine whether a victim's blood is present. Crime scene evidence can be compared to blood samples taken from a suspect, or it can be compared to a computerized database of DNA "fingerprints." States maintain their own databases of the DNA profiles of convicted felons, and the Federal Bureau of Investigation (FBI) operates a national database called the Combined DNA Index System (CODIS). All of this is made possible using technology in constant development since the mid-1980s, which allows scientists to examine tiny segments of DNA.

Although each person's DNA is different (except pairs of identical twins), there are many similarities between different people's DNA. For example, each person's DNA contains certain regions consisting of short segments that are repeated a varying number of times. One person might have 120 copies of the segment, and someone else might have 125. By examining these regions, scientists are able to compare DNA from two sources—such as crime scene evidence and a blood sample—and if the two samples contain different numbers of copies of the segment, then it can be determined that the DNA came from different sources.

In essence, then, a scientist wishing to conduct a DNA test must seek out a particular region of DNA and count how many copies of the segment there are. To do such a test, it is necessary to tear apart the DNA molecule using chemicals called restriction enzymes, which essentially seek out a particular portion of the DNA strand and cut it. The fragments of the DNA strands can then be identified using chemicals called DNA probes, which themselves are actually short fragments of DNA strands, together with a radioactive atom or chemical dye, that will bind to the specific fragments of DNA being tested. The radioactivity or dye allows the counting of the number of segments. Using a restriction enzyme to cut DNA into fragments and measure their length is referred to as Restriction Fragment Length Poly-morphism (RFLP) technology: Polymorphism means having various forms (or in this case, number of repetitions).

Alec Jeffreys used RFLP technology to do the DNA tests in the Pitchfork case. He relied on regions of DNA having segments that were repeated several hundred times. The chance that two people would have the same number of segments was small, but when six regions of DNA were tested, the chances that two people would have the same number of segments in all six regions was miniscule. For example, the chance that two white people living in the United States would match in all six regions is about one in 100 billion.[1] Being able to show this type of probability when comparing crime scene evidence to a blood sample has obvious value in law enforcement. RFLP technology, however, has several significant disadvantages. Because the process involves breaking down the DNA molecules, a large sample of DNA is needed, and RFLP cannot detect trace amounts of DNA, on a toothpick for instance, nor can it be used to test crime scene samples that have degraded over time. Additionally, the process of testing several regions of the DNA could take days or even weeks.

As police began collecting DNA evidence from increasing numbers of crime scenes and became eager to use DNA in more and more cases, they needed a procedure that was quicker and could be performed on smaller, or partially degraded, DNA samples. The answer came with the development of Polymerase Chain Reaction (PCR) technology. PCR is not a new type of test; rather, it is a method for replicating strands of DNA. It has essentially the same effect as a copy machine. After breaking

DNA strands into fragments, PCR allows a scientist to make multiple copies of the fragment. The process, however, could not be used with the relatively large fragments tested in conventional RFLP analysis in use at the time. PCR only worked on much smaller fragments. Scientists, however, soon developed tests for locations that could be replicated.

The first PCR-based test used in forensic science, called DQ alpha, had a major disadvantage in comparison to RFLP: Its results were much less conclusive. Although the test was good at excluding people, it was not very good at implicating people. As much as 5 percent of the population could produce the same results. Scientists developed PCR-based tests for five additional locations in 1993, but the tests were still nowhere near as conclusive as the RFLP tests, with the new tests having about a one in four thousand chance of a random match.[2]

- **What type of odds should be required for conviction "beyond a reasonable doubt"?**

The breakthrough came with the development of short tandem repeat (STR) testing. Essentially, STR testing works a lot like the older RFLP testing, but measures much shorter segments—segments that are short enough to be replicated using PCR. Another advantage to the STR technology is that segments from numerous regions could be replicated at the same time. This process, called multiplexing, made testing faster. The FBI selected thirteen STR regions to be used as the standard for DNA testing. If all thirteen loci (the position of a particular gene or allele in a chromosome), are tested the chance of a random match between two unrelated white people in the United States is about one in 575 trillion.[3]

It should be noted that none of the forensic DNA tests focus on the portion of the DNA in which genes are located. Rather, they focus on junk DNA that reveals no information about an individual. The sole exception is that some testing indicates the sex of the person whose DNA is being tested. This test, however, is considered useful for investigating rape cases, in which a given sample might contain the DNA of both the victim and the rapist.

Controversies in DNA Testing and Evidence

When the police called on Colin Pitchfork, he realized that his back was against the wall. Since then, thousands of other people have also felt that way, thanks to DNA testing. While the usefulness of DNA in solving crimes cannot reasonably be disputed, its use by law enforcement officials has spawned many controversies. The method employed by the English police in the Pitchfork case—asking all men in the small villages to provide DNA samples—is a perfect example. Why should innocent people be asked to provide their DNA to the police? Perhaps some people would be perfectly willing to do so, but others are not so sure. Although the police test only for identification purposes, they have a sample of DNA that could conceivably be tested for other purposes. Privacy advocates do not think that the government should be snooping into anyone's genetic makeup, let alone that of innocent citizens. Law enforcement officials, however, have been rapidly increasing the numbers of people from whom DNA samples are being taken, and some people have even called for everyone in the nation to provide DNA samples.

Even as law enforcement officials are relying more and more on DNA testing, some people continue to question whether DNA testing is really as conclusive as it is made out to be. When prosecutors present odds in the billions or trillions that anyone other than the defendant could be guilty, does the defendant really have any chance of acquittal? What happens if there is a mistake in the DNA testing? What if the sample was contaminated with the defendant's blood during testing, as was alleged in O. J. Simpson's murder trial? What if the DNA was planted? With odds like that, framing someone appears easy.

• **Can police be trusted not to misuse DNA samples?**

With law enforcement officials collecting blood and saliva samples from hundreds of thousands of people, some people are not confident that law enforcement officials will use that information just for identification purposes. Unlike the ridges and whirls of a fingerprint, DNA contains all kinds of information that researchers might find useful. Is there a gene that causes violence? Are people of certain racial backgrounds more likely to commit crimes because of their genetic makeup? Some researchers want to know answers to these questions, but privacy advocates oppose this type of research as a misuse of information taken supposedly for identification alone.

As DNA testing becomes more widely available, it is being used to reexamine old cases. DNA testing takes time and money, however, and there is considerable debate about which old cases should receive priority. Already, a number of people who were convicted by juries have been exonerated after DNA tests showed that someone else committed the crime, and now thousands of convicted offenders are calling for DNA tests. But how many of these people are actually innocent? After all, they had the opportunity for a jury trial. Crime victims and their families believe that the justice system should focus its efforts instead in performing DNA tests on the hundreds of thousands of pieces of untested crime scene evidence, as well as getting as many criminals' DNA profiles entered into computer databases as possible.

Summary

As DNA technology has become more advanced, police and prosecutors have become more aggressive in using it in criminal cases. Its use, however, has generated controversy because of the deeply personal nature of taking a person's DNA. At the same time, its use has also pointed out flaws in the criminal justice system that have led to wrongful convictions.

Prosecutors Overstate the Reliability of DNA Evidence

Walking down the street one day in 1998, teenager Josiah Sutton and a friend were arrested after a woman pointed them out to police as the two men who had raped her several days earlier. Sutton and his friend were shocked, and they proclaimed their innocence. They assumed that when they provided DNA samples, their names would be cleared. Sutton's friend was released after a DNA test failed to match him to the crime scene evidence. The reports from the Houston Police Department's crime lab, however, stated that Sutton's DNA was consistent with the crime scene evidence, and that only one in 694,000 people had the matching characteristics. With those types of odds, a jury convicted Sutton and sentenced him to twenty-five years in prison. All along, Sutton maintained his innocence.

Sutton's appeals were going nowhere until a Houston television station broke the news that the Houston crime lab was having some serious problems. A pair of reporters, acting on tips from defense lawyers, had launched an investigation into the crime lab and had sent some of the lab's reports to independent experts. Those experts found serious flaws in the lab's work. Sutton's mother happened to see this story on the news, and she contacted the reporters to tell them about her son's case. The reporters sent his case files to a prominent DNA expert who had been part of O. J. Simpson's "dream team" of defense lawyers in the former football star's murder trial. William Thompson discovered that the crime lab had misinterpreted the results of the DNA tests, and that, in fact, Sutton's DNA was inconsistent with the DNA of either of the two rapists. After a new DNA test of crime scene evidence confirmed Thompson's conclusions, Sutton was finally freed from prison, after four years behind bars for a crime that he did not commit.

Cases like Sutton's raise serious questions about the validity of the DNA evidence presented by prosecution witnesses. At his original trial, Sutton did not have the benefit of a "dream team" of DNA experts to challenge the crime lab's faulty conclusions. In Simpson's trial, by contrast, defense attorneys successfully attacked the validity of DNA evidence taken from the crime scene, Simpson's house, and his truck by suggesting that evidence had been planted or was contaminated during testing. After Simpson's acquittal, many people were left with the impression that DNA evidence is easily challenged in court; however, that is not the case. Because of the complex nature of DNA evidence, challenging its validity requires expert witnesses and defense lawyers who are familiar with the issues. Unfortunately, such expertise comes at a very high cost, and unlike O. J. Simpson, most criminal defendants simply cannot afford such expertise.

As a result of the expense involved, the validity of a DNA test is rarely challenged in court. Defense attorney Chris Plourd remarked:

I get a call once a week on a case, on cases from around the country and the question is always the same. We want to fight this DNA test. I'm very excited. I say, oh, that's wonderful. Send me $350,000, because that's about what it takes to do a scientific validity test when you're hiring experts and you're going to have six to eight weeks of a hearing and hire every prominent expert in the country. Well, obviously, the test doesn't get done.[4]

Josiah Sutton was very lucky that his case was reviewed, but he never should have been convicted. Many wonder how many other people have been wrongfully convicted after juries hear staggering odds that anyone beside the defendant could be the culprit. Yet prosecutors continue to push for using newer DNA technologies that present even higher odds and retrieve DNA from weaker and weaker sources. Some people have even called for removing the question of DNA tests' validity from juries' hands, instead letting judges instruct jurors that a DNA match has been found. Many defense attorneys and scholars, however, believe these steps are all going a little too far and would like to urge caution in the use of DNA evidence to convict.

Crime labs make errors in testing and presenting DNA evidence.

Frequently prosecutors introduce DNA evidence in criminal trials in a manner that makes any challenge seem insurmountable. Typically, the prosecutor will call a scientist as an expert witness, who will then give an opinion as to whether the DNA from the crime scene matches the defendant's DNA. This opinion is typically given by stating the odds that the crime scene DNA could belong to anyone other than the defendant, and these odds are frequently presented as one in millions, or even billions. Some experts believe, however, that presenting such odds can be very misleading. Because crime labs make occasional errors, Professor Laurence Mueller has argued, the probability should be presented in a manner that reflects the likely error rate. He wrote:

[It] would be appropriate to use 1 in 1 million to weight a DNA match [only] in a laboratory in which the rate of error was demonstrably less than 1 in 1 million. . . . [but] evidence suggests that rates of false matches are in the range of 1 in hundreds to 1 in thousands. To present a jury with a very rare random match probability vastly overstates the weight which should be accorded a single DNA match.[5]

Even in laboratories with no documented errors, he explains, the error rate cannot be declared accurately to be zero, or even less than one in a billion. The problem with such claims is that laboratories have not conducted a billion tests, and therefore there is no way of knowing that an error would only occur in one out of every one billion tests.

One source of error is contamination of samples. DNA testing is an extremely sensitive procedure, capable of detecting even a single copy of DNA. DNA is easily transferred from object to object, or from a person to an object. If DNA is transferred to a piece of evidence either while being handled by police or while being tested in the laboratory, it can create false impressions. For example, a victim's DNA could be transferred to an item that was in the possession of the suspect, or the suspect's DNA could be transferred to evidence taken from the crime scene. In either case, the resulting tests would falsely implicate the suspect, and therefore, extreme caution is needed when handling DNA evidence.

In the O. J. Simpson trial, prosecutors introduced evidence that they said conclusively linked Simpson to the murders of Nicole Brown Simpson and Ronald Goldman, notably evidence found at the crime scene, which prosecutors said contained Simpson's blood, and evidence from Simpson's car and home, which prosecutors said contained the victims' blood. The defense, however, challenged the validity of the evidence. A laboratory worker for the Los Angeles Police Department (LAPD) performed DNA tests on a vial of blood taken from Simpson as a reference just before performing tests on evidence taken from the crime scene. While opening the vial of Simpson's blood, the worker spilled some of Simpson's blood on his latex glove, which he discarded. However, defense witness Dr. John Gerdes criticized these procedures because they resulted in a high risk that Simpson's blood would contaminate the crime scene evidence.

> • **Do you believe that O. J. Simpson was not responsible for the murders? Do you believe he was framed by police?**

Another source of error is mislabeling samples, either in the laboratory or when reporting the results. In a rape trial in 1995, an expert witness from Cellmark Laboratories showed illustrations of the DNA samples taken from the rape kit, from the suspect's DNA test, and from the victim's DNA test. She initially testified that the DNA from the rape kit matched the suspect's DNA test; however, during the trial she realized that the labels on the diagrams of the suspect's and the victim's DNA had been switched. Rather than showing that the DNA from the rape kit matched the suspect's DNA, it actually showed that it matched the victim's DNA, which was only natural and said absolutely nothing about the suspect's guilt.

Witnesses can also misinterpret the results of tests, as happened in Josiah Sutton's case. The Houston crime lab concluded that a stain taken from the victim's car contained DNA from the victim and two others, including Sutton. When William Thompson reviewed the lab's conclusions, however, he reached a different result: The sample came from a single person, and Sutton's DNA had a marker that was not included in the sample. When Thompson reviewed the test results for the other samples, they also did not include Sutton's DNA. Everything in the lab report necessary to exonerate Sutton was there in black and white. Thompson told *60 Minutes II*, "I think that the Houston Police Lab has personnel that are not particularly competent, who are working under situations where they have incentives to distort their findings in favor of the police and prosecution."[6]

California v. Kocak

Cellmark laboratories has performed DNA tests in the trial of John Kocak, who is accused of raping A. F. Earlier in the trial, this witness, an employee of Cellmark, has testified that the odds are remote that the DNA sample retrieved from the crime scene could match anyone other than Kocak. However, after a break in the trial, the witness returns to the stand with a startling revelation.

The Court: This report has an error in it [?]

The Witness: I think so. I'm a little hysterical right now, but I think the—according to our log sheet, our sample 02 would be the known sample for Mr. Kocak. The—our sample 03 is the known sample from Miss F. And in explaining the gel earlier, it—I realized that the analysis . . . we had done, which shows that the sample 03 is consistent with the types from sample 01A, is correct, but what we incorrectly reported is that 03 was Mr. Kocak's sample. . . . So if you go to our report page 2, the types detected results chart, the types are all correct, but the two names should be switched. And then the conclusions would be incorrect, that the data—the primary data that we have obtained are consistent with the types from Miss F., and we can make no conclusion regarding the faint bands, which may or may not include Mr. Kocak. . . .

The Court: . . . I don't mean to beat a dead horse, but I need to understand, on page 2 of the June 23 report, how this would be changed to reflect what you believe to be the accurate data. What would you mark out and change? . . .

The Witness: . . . [In the conclusion section,] all the names should also be changed. Where it says, "A. F. is excluded as the source," it should say John Kocak is excluded as the source. Where it says, "John Kocak cannot be excluded," it should . . . say "A. F. cannot be excluded." And then the frequency calculations would all be for A. F., not for Mr. Kocak. . . .

Source: Trial Transcript, *People of California* v. *John Ivan Kocak*, No. SCD110465 (Nov. 17, 1995).

As technology advances, prosecutors rush untested methods into court.

When police first began using DNA evidence to catch criminals, and prosecutors first began using it to try suspects, many were skeptical about whether DNA technology could be trusted. Other types of crime scene evidence, such as fingerprints and bullets, required some form of expertise in order to interpret. For example, a fingerprint expert could establish the similarity between a suspect's fingerprints and those taken from the crime scene. Similarly, a ballistics expert could testify how tests of a gun linked to the suspect revealed markings on the bullet identical to the one taken from the crime scene. With these types of evidence, however, the members of the jury could see the

FROM THE BENCH

Colorado v. *Schreck* (Trial Court Ruling)

In a decision later overturned by the Colorado Supreme Court, the trial judge expressed skepticism about the accuracy of a new automated DNA testing system.

STR's are multiple copies of an identical DNA sequence arranged in direct succession in a particular region of a chromosome. These sequences are widespread throughout the human genome and show sufficient variability among individuals in a population that they have become important in human identity testing. The forensic DNA community has embraced the use of STRs which may be amplified with PCR with greater fidelity than other repeats. The STR loci provide a rich source of polymorphic markers and their use provides a high degree of discrimination....

STR testing has been used for research and medical diagnostics for over eight years. It is used to detect residual disease after bone marrow transplants, in parentage assessment and cell line authentication. It has been used forensically since about 1993 in Europe, Canada and the United States.

When STR loci are amplified separately and run on a separate gel, the system is called "monoplex". When the loci are amplified together and run in one gel lane or capillary injection simultaneously, the system is called "multiplex". Multiplex similarities with their own eyes. DNA, by contrast, is microscopic, and juries are asked to put a great deal of faith in the prosecution witness who testifies to the existence of DNA traces and the likelihood of a match.

After some period of skepticism, however, methods for extracting and comparing DNA gained more widespread acceptance, and courts throughout the nation began accepting DNA evidence more or less without question. In general, a court will admit scientific evidence under one of two standards. Some courts admit scientific evidence if it is based upon methods "generally accepted" by the scientific community. Other courts admit scientific evidence that the judges deem is reliable based on factors such as whether it has been widely studied and how

systems that amplify and run three loci, or "triplex" systems, have been available commercially since 1993, and both monoplex and triplex systems have been in use for many years. . . .

The multiplex system at issue in this case is a combination nineplex and sixplex system. The People contend that this is merely another application of the already scientifically accepted STR method. . . . The Defense argues that the testing using new loci and new primers in one procedure changes the method to such an extent and presents new problems such that it must be considered a novel scientific process. . . .

The FBI has invested a great deal of money and time on this system as have the laboratories that purchased the kits. There is great incentive to prove their reliability. They will probably be found reliable after the shortcomings noted above are addressed. However, "probably reliable" is not the standard for admissibility in a court of law. The Court understands that, in this rapidly changing field, the time frame in which acceptance is evidenced may be accelerated, especially where market competition drives the technology. But, where a defendant's freedom is at stake, market competition is no substitute for good science.

Source: *People of Colorado* v. *Michael Eugene Schreck*, No. 98CR2475 (Dist. Ct. Colorado 2000).

reliable testing methods are. Under either of these two standards, courts have regularly admitted testimony about DNA matches.

- **Should prosecutors be limited to technologies that have been around for a while?**

DNA technology began to change rapidly, however, as police and prosecutors began employing technology that was able to extract DNA from sources that could not previously be tested, such as sources in which the DNA had partly degraded or samples with very little DNA present. Other technology helped scientists establish a higher likelihood of a match or allowed them to perform the tests more quickly. Defense attorneys believe that often prosecutors have rushed to embrace these new technologies before they really can be trusted to provide reliable results. Such a challenge would be critical in cases in which previous technologies were unable to extract DNA from evidence or provided a less conclusive match to the defendant.

Recently, defense attorneys have had only limited success in challenging the application of new DNA technologies, such as multiplexing PCR technology. The PCR process is used to copy pieces of DNA being tested, much like a photocopy machine, and multiplexing technology allows the laboratory to copy multiple DNA markers at the same time. (The standard DNA "fingerprint" used by the FBI includes thirteen distinct markers, or portions of DNA that vary greatly from person to person.) When multiplexing technology was first used in court, defense lawyers around the nation challenged its use, saying that the technology was unproven, and therefore might produce errors. Trial courts in Vermont and Colorado upheld the challenges and refused to admit tests based on the new technology; however, the Colorado Supreme Court overruled the Colorado trial court's decision. The court in Vermont noted:

> [This multiplexing test kit] has not been subject to scrutiny through articles in peer-reviewed journals. There have been

no independent validation studies. . . . Without the scrutiny of the scientific community, the Court cannot establish whether [the kit] is a reliable system, or one prone to error. Regardless of whether the technique is generally accepted in the commercial forensic community or is widely used in building convicted offender databases, no appellate court has found that this system is validated for use in a criminal proceeding.[7]

Juries should decide for themselves whether to believe the DNA evidence.

During the O. J. Simpson trial, numerous legal observers who believed that Simpson had committed the murders with which he had been charged were incensed when he was found not guilty by the jury. These critics said that the jury had not understood the weight of the DNA evidence presented by the prosecution, and some even called for taking the question of DNA evidence out of the hands of the jury. In the opinion of some, the judge should decide in a separate hearing whether the DNA evidence presented by the prosecution indicated a DNA match with the defendant.

• **Do juries need to understand the science behind DNA testing for a defendant to get a fair trial?**

Such proposals, however, ignore the importance of jury trials in the American system of justice. The Sixth Amendment to the U.S. Constitution states:

In all criminal prosecutions, the accused shall enjoy the right to a speedy and public trial, by an impartial jury of the state and district wherein the crime shall have been committed, . . . and to be informed of the nature and cause of the accusation; to be confronted with the witnesses against him; to have compulsory process for obtaining witnesses in his favor, and to have the assistance of counsel for his defense.[8]

Additionally, the involvement of juries helps to place a check on the actions of prosecutors and police officers. Simpson's attorneys won his acquittal primarily by attacking the methods

California v. Simpson

Defense attorneys called Dr. John Gerdes to the stand to explain how a lab technician could have contaminated critical pieces of evidence with blood drawn from O. J. Simpson for the purpose of comparing his DNA to the crime scene evidence. The technician tested Simpson's blood in the same laboratory and on the same day that he tested these pieces of evidence.

MR. SCHECK: Now . . . what is your opinion of this laboratory practice of handling Mr. Simpson's reference tubes [of blood] in the way Mr. Yamauchi described it and these evidence samples [leather gloves and blood drops] within that period? . . .

DR. GERDES: That is not an acceptable practice in any forensic laboratory . . . [because] of the unacceptable risk of contamination from the reference sample which has high levels of DNA and the evidence items that were processed which have low levels. . . .

MR. SCHECK: Now, you read Mr. Yamauchi's testimony where you indicated that after he opened the reference tube and the blood went through his chem wipe and went onto his [latex laboratory] glove that he then disposed of the [latex] gloves. . . . Now, given the nature of his testimony about the way he opened the tube, do you think that what he did next in terms of moving onto the analysis of the other sample was an acceptable laboratory practice?

DR. GERDES: No. [If] you've had a spillage, you should have basically stopped everything, cleaned down the entire lab and waited for a period of time before you move on to something as critical as evidence items.

Source: Trial Transcript, *People of California v. O. J. Simpson* (August 2, 1995). Available online at *http://simpson.walraven.org/aug02.html*.

of the police officers, whom the defense portrayed as sloppy and eager to convict. As defense attorney Chris Plourd observed:

> The evidence in the Simpson case was extremely strong, but it was an attack based upon mishandling and . . . the jury reacted to that. They didn't trust the police officers. Well, they grew up with those police officers, and essentially, the attorneys in that case were preaching to the choir because they were willing to accept something that they live with their whole lives.[9]

Because juries are much less predictable than judges, police and prosecutors have great incentive to make sure that evidence handling and testing procedures are as careful as possible. In Houston, for example, once the news broke about widespread problems at the crime lab, jurors expressed skepticism about the validity of evidence presented by prosecutors. As evidenced by Josiah Sutton's case, mistakes do happen, and the police department was forced to make wholesale changes in its crime lab in order to maintain the public trust, because juries are made up of members of the public.

Summary

The case of Josiah Sutton, who was wrongfully convicted, serves as a reminder that DNA evidence is not infallible. Even though prosecution witnesses frequently present testimony that the DNA evidence is an overwhelming indicator of guilt, the evidence is collected by humans, who sometimes make mistakes and sometimes even lie. Because DNA evidence is often presented as conclusive, defense attorneys believe that it is important to use only well-tested technologies and to allow juries to prove whether the collection and testing methods are reliable.

DNA Evidence Provides a Reliable Basis for Convictions

Once considered futuristic technology, DNA evidence has become increasingly reliable, say its advocates. Improvements have occurred rapidly, allowing the testing of smaller amounts of material, faster testing procedures, and more conclusive results. These improvements have not only helped law enforcement, but have improved the accuracy of the court system's fact-finding process.

Terry Hillard, superintendent of the Chicago Police Department, is a firm believer that DNA technology has become an extremely accurate indicator of innocence or guilt. While speaking to a group of law enforcement officials in 2000, he gave an example of just how much technology has improved, and how much this improvement has helped the justice system.[10] In 1985, a legal secretary was murdered in Austin, Texas. Police suspected an ex-convict who had just visited the law firm where the victim worked, but they had little evidence to link him to the crime. The type of blood testing in use at the time, serology, only identified a person's blood type—A, B, AB, or O. Although it could be used to exclude innocent people, when serology produced a match, as it did in this case, the results were not very helpful, because significant percentages of the population share blood types. The authorities could not charge the suspect, but the detective in charge of the case did not forget about it.

In 1989, the detective saw a ray of hope when DNA testing became available, but the type of technology (RFLP) in use at the time required a large amount of fresh DNA to produce results, and the evidence remaining from the case produced no results. However, when PCR, the technology that allows small amounts of DNA to be replicated, became widely available in 1993, the stubborn detective sent the samples in again, hoping that this time, the testing would produce results. Unfortunately, it did not, because the tests (DQ alpha) at the time only examined certain areas of the DNA, and the suspect had a fairly common profile. It would take much more sensitive tests to yield useful results.

When STR testing became available, it provided the results that the detective had been hoping for. The first test that was conducted looked at nine locations, and it indicated that there was about a one in ten thousand chance of a random match between the suspect and the crime scene evidence. Although persuasive, the detective did not think that it would hold up in court, so he sent the evidence to another lab that had started analyzing for the thirteen locations specified by the FBI for its CODIS database. The detective finally had what he needed: The chances of a random match were less than one in a million, and the suspect was finally charged with the murder and was facing trial when Hillard spoke.

Many prosecutors, scientists, police officers, politicians, and others stand firmly behind DNA testing. They believe that the testing is extremely accurate. Although errors are possible, they are rare, and can be discovered in the trial or appeals process. Despite efforts to cast suspicion on DNA testing, advocates say that it is much more reliable than other forms of evidence, and juries should not be swayed into rejecting this now well-established technology.

> • **How can an innocent defendant contest DNA evidence in the face of overwhelming odds?**

DNA testing is based on sound science, and errors are rare.

Although defense attorneys for a time vigorously challenged the validity of DNA evidence, such challenges have become increasingly less likely to succeed as courts realize that DNA technology is here to stay. As Henry Lee and Frank Tirnady explain in their book *Blood Evidence: How DNA is Revolutionizing the Way We Solve Crimes,* "The stuff works. The real weakness of forensic DNA analysis, just as with any other legitimate forensic technique, is not *what* is being done, but *how* it is being done, and by whom."[11] Although errors are possible, as is shown by the experience with the Houston crime lab's misinterpretation of evidence in the rape conviction of Josiah Sutton, these errors are few and far between. Although it was initially expected that the investigation of the Houston crime lab would turn up numerous faulty DNA analyses, this did not turn out to be the case.

In fact, errors in processing DNA evidence are rare. The few that have been identified have been identified because they *can* be identified. Unlike other forms of evidence, such as eyewitness testimony, DNA evidence can be reviewed, as happened in the Sutton case. The National Research Council and the National Institute of Justice have rejected the idea that the probability of laboratory errors should be considered in calculating the probability of a DNA match, suggesting instead that evidence about errors be weighed against the probability of a match, and that defendants should have the opportunity to conduct their own DNA tests. According to the National Institute of Justice, "[W]henever possible only a part of the evidence material [should] be used for analysis and the rest retained for future use. With PCR methods it is very unlikely that the entire evidence DNA is consumed in the analysis. . . . [The] best protection for a suspect who may have been wrongly accused because of an error is the opportunity for an independent retest." [12]

FROM THE BENCH

Mississippi Court Rejects Vague Allegations of Contamination

[The defendant's] expert, Dr. Acton, focused on the susceptibility to contamination inherent in the PCR amplification process. Dr. Sinha and Pat Wojtikieiac, however, explained the controls in the laboratory process which are designed to identify— and minimize—any instances of contamination. Deborah Haller further demon- strated the precautions taken by the State Crime Lab to safeguard against contamination of the samples prepared for the genetic laboratory.

Watts, however, attempts to bolster his case by misconstruing evidence and mischaracterizing witness testimony in the record, speculating where contam- ination might have occurred. . . . He . . . suggests that the victim's blood may have been present on his jacket because Sam Howell, Chief of Toxicology at the Mississippi Crime Lab, assisted Dr. Ward with the autopsy one day and the next, collected three items of evidence, including the jacket! While this raises matters of Mr. Howell's personal hygiene that were not made part of the record, his contention is also refuted by Deborah Haller's testimony regarding the rigorous protocol followed to avoid contamination in the crime lab.

This Court has found that PCR testing of DNA samples produces reliable results in a forensic setting. The record contains no evidence of error in the process of collecting and testing the DNA evidence in this case. We therefore do not find the circuit court to be in error for denying Watts' motion to suppress the evidence.

Source: *Watts* v. *State*, 733 So. 2d 214 (Mississippi 1999)

It is not just prosecutors and law-and-order advocates who support the use of DNA testing in criminal courts: Even some advocates for the rights of the accused have been forced to acknowledge the reliability of DNA evidence. While remaining concerned about some of the privacy-related aspects of DNA testing, Peter Neufeld of the Innocence Project in New York, which helps prisoners challenge their convictions, testified to Congress:

[M]any other so called "forensic science" disciplines utilized routinely by state and local law enforcement agencies . . . lack the validity, reliability and internal controls inherent in DNA technology. Since most serious crimes lack relevant biological evidence, law enforcement investigations rely more on the crime lab's non-DNA disciplines such as ballistics, handwriting comparison, hair and fiber analysis, tool marks and finger-prints to decide whether or not to prosecute. None of these forensic disciplines enjoys the heightened scientific dimension of DNA. That is why post-conviction DNA testing has had unparalleled success in correcting miscarriages of justice. The genetic results are often simply indisputable.[13]

Neufeld gave the example as support for the argument that people convicted of crimes before the widespread availability of DNA testing should have the opportunity to have their cases reexamined. Ironically, before Neufeld became well known for promoting the use of DNA testing to prove innocence, he was well known for challenging the validity of DNA in court. Some people believe that defense attorneys, in their overzealous protection of the rights of the accused, seem to want a double standard when it comes to DNA evidence. Arizona Judge Ronald Reinstein noted, "It is interesting to observe how quickly some DNA-evidence opponents embrace the science when it benefits certain defendants' interests but how defensive they become when the evidence points *toward* other defendants."[14]

DNA evidence is more reliable than many traditional forms of evidence.

While some defense attorneys question the reliability of DNA evidence, many legal experts consider DNA evidence to be one of the most reliable forms of evidence available. Mistakes do happen, as was the case in Josiah Sutton's erroneous rape conviction, but they are much less likely to happen than with other types of evidence. As a case in point, when Josiah Sutton was convicted of rape, the jury was presented not only with DNA evidence, but with the victim's identification of Sutton as the rapist. While the average lay person might assume that having an eyewitness identify a suspect is the most reliable form of evidence possible, experts say otherwise. Columbia law professor Michael Dorf states that as many as 50 percent of eyewitness identifications are erroneous, a statistic he calls "frightening" in the light of the many convictions based mostly on eyewitness testimony. He wrote:

> [S]tudies show . . . that the ability to identify a stranger is diminished by stress (and what crime situation is not intensely stressful?), that cross-racial identifications are especially unreliable, and that contrary to what one might think, those witnesses who claim to be "certain" of their identifications are no better at it than everyone else, just more confident.[15]

- **Does a handful of wrongful convictions justify a large number of crimes being solved with DNA evidence?**

In some circumstances, DNA evidence might even be more reliable than a confession. Testifying before Congress, attorney Peter Neufeld told the story of Earl Washington, a man with an IQ of sixty-nine, who was arrested on burglary charges, and after two days of interrogation, confessed to five other crimes. Prosecutors did not pursue charges in four of the cases, because the victims in those cases did not identify Washington as responsible. However, says Neufeld, because "the fifth victim was no longer alive to prove his confession false," prosecutors pursued charges even though his so-called confession was riddled with inconsistencies. Neufeld testified:

> Although Washington reportedly "confessed" that he raped and killed Rebecca Lynn Williams, subsequent questioning revealed that Washington did not know the race of his victim, the address of the apartment where she was killed or that he had [supposedly] sexually assaulted her. Washington described Ms. Williams as short when, in fact, she was 5'8", that he had stabbed her two or three times although the stab wounds on the victim's body numbered thirty-eight, and that there was no one else in the apartment when it was known that Ms. Williams' young children were in the apartment with her on the day of the crime. Only on the fourth attempt at a rehearsed confession did authorities accept Washington's statement and have it recorded in writing with Washington's signature. Washington was able to pick out the scene of the crime only after being taken there three times in one afternoon by the police who, in the end, had to help him pick out Williams' apartment. The confession proved to be the prosecution's only evidence linking Washington to the crime.[16]

Nevertheless, Washington was sent to prison for the crime, and it was only after a subsequent DNA test on the ample crime scene evidence that Washington was exonerated because his DNA did not match.

Discounting DNA evidence is not a proper function for the jury.

Although some people applauded the Simpson acquittal as the vindication of an innocent man incriminated by DNA evidence that was either mishandled or planted, many experts say that the members of the jury simply did not understand the evidence facing Simpson, and that they were swayed by emotion rather than logic. Vincent Bugliosi, who prosecuted serial killer Charles Manson, remarked:

> Whenever I caught a snippet of the DNA testimony, with its extremely complex genetic, molecular, and statistical principles . . . I wondered how the jury, particularly the seventy-year-old . . . woman who . . . never read the newspaper or anything at all except the Racing Form, and had difficulty following even it, could have followed what they were talking about.[17]

The presentation of DNA evidence at trial is indeed very complicated. Although some states have eliminated the requirement of background testimony about DNA testing, in most cases, the prosecution must introduce expert witnesses, who must testify as to their own expertise with DNA, give general testimony as to how DNA testing works, and explain how the tests were done in the case being tried. The expert witness must then explain how the results are compared to population data to determine the odds that the DNA match could be the result

THE LETTER OF THE LAW

Minnesota's Law on the Admissibility of DNA Evidence

In a civil or criminal trial or hearing, the results of DNA analysis . . . are admissible in evidence without antecedent expert testimony that DNA analysis provides a trustworthy and reliable method of identifying characteristics in an individual's genetic material upon a showing that the offered testimony meets the standards for admissibility set forth in the Rules of Evidence.

Source: Minn. Stat. § 634.25 (2004).

of a random match rather than the result of the defendant's DNA being present at the crime scene. In most trials in which DNA evidence is used, therefore, a significant amount of scientific testimony is presented.

Some people have suggested that the process of introducing DNA evidence is unnecessarily burdensome. In essence, what is happening is that the same basic information is being presented in every trial, and that the net result is rather simple: whether the defendant's DNA was found at the crime scene (or whether the victim's DNA was linked to the defendant). Judge Ronald Reinstein has argued, "experts should be able to testify . . . whether one evidence sample matches another to a reasonable degree of scientific certainty. There is a serious question about whether DNA-match testimony should be treated any differently from that of fingerprints, bite marks, hair and fiber samples, ballistics, shoe prints, and the like."[18] Legislators in states including Minnesota agree, having dispensed with the requirement that experts justify the validity of DNA evidence in every trial.

> • **Should jurors be allowed to act on their own distrust of scientific methods?**

In a law review article, Ryan McDonald went even further, suggesting the use of a separate DNA hearing, without the jury present and before the main trial begins. At the hearing, the prosecution would present evidence about the testing procedures used and the test results, but would not have to present as much background information because the judge or the judge's staff would have a working knowledge of DNA issues. The defense would be able to present information about possible mishandling of evidence or improper testing procedures. The judge would then rule on whether the collection and testing of evidence met the required standards; if so, the judge would simply instruct the jury that a DNA match existed, and if not, the judge would instruct the jury that no DNA match existed. The advantages to such a system would be "faster, more efficient, more reliable [jury] deliberations" because the members of the jury would not be sidetracked by complicated DNA issues, and "a frame of reference" for appeals courts, which would only have to determine whether the judge erred in finding that the handling of the evidence did or did not comply with acceptable standards.[19]

Summary

Although defense attorneys still criticize DNA evidence as "junk science" when it points to their clients, there is little doubt that DNA identification is a well-established discipline. Improvements in technology have made the tests more accurate and capable of producing almost indisputable evidence of guilt. In the extremely rare cases in which errors are made, the answer is to do an independent test, not to challenge the technology itself. In fact, DNA evidence is probably the most reliable form of evidence, and many people believe that it is not a proper function of the jury to reject sound science.

Collecting DNA Samples Threatens Privacy

It is impossible at this stage to deny the usefulness of DNA evidence in investigating crimes. Civil libertarians, however, argue that its usefulness does not tell the whole story. Many people fear that the collection of DNA will replace traditional police work, in which detectives search for evidence that links a particular person to a crime, such as whether the person matches a description of the suspect, or whether someone else has implicated the person in the crime. The use of DNA matching, civil libertarians argue, allows police to target an individual even when no evidence links him or her to the crime, because the police know that if they can match a DNA sample, they can build a case.

In general, the Constitution's Bill of Rights protects citizens from police harassment. The Fourth Amendment, in particular, states:

> The right of the people to be secure in their persons, houses,
> papers, and effects, against unreasonable searches and
> seizures, shall not be violated, and no warrants shall issue,
> but upon probable cause, supported by oath or affirmation,
> and particularly describing the place to be searched, and the
> persons or things to be seized.[20]

Traditionally, a person cannot be arrested, and his or her home cannot be searched, unless the police have "probable cause" to suspect that a person has committed a crime. This requirement of probable cause extends to requiring someone to provide a DNA sample, which is a "seizure" of a most personal nature. However, as illustrated by the following story recounted by Terry Gainer, executive assistant chief of police for the District of Columbia, police can simply follow a hunch and then hound a person in search of his or her DNA:

> This is a case which was a sexual assault. The detectives felt
> that they had narrowed down a suspect, but still couldn't tie
> the suspect to the case. They did not have enough probable
> cause to get a warrant to get any biological samples from
> the suspect.
>
> What they creatively did was, in happenstance, following
> the offender one day saw this offender spit a nice hocker . . .
> on the street. . . . What those detectives, with the use of a
> bit of serendipity, did was get out a Kleenex, bend down
> and pick up that spit, took it in and processed it to the
> crime lab and lo and behold, the truth of the matter is the
> DNA from that sample matched up to the offender and
> they solved the case.[21]

Chief Gainer praised this police work. In this particular case, the hunch of the police happened to be correct, and the suspect had committed a criminal act. However, civil libertarians are concerned about a future in which police can follow a person around, waiting for the person to spit on the sidewalk or throw a used tissue or a piece of gum in the trash so that the officers can collect genetic material—information that not only can link the person to unsolved crimes, but could also reveal information about familial relationships or the likelihood of developing a deadly disease. Without requiring probable cause for collecting DNA samples, police conceivably could target people of a particular race, religion, or political party.

> • **When you throw away a piece of gum or a drinking straw, do you expect that police will confiscate it for scientific testing?**

The process of collecting DNA samples is invasive.

To some people, having genetic information taken is one of the most intrusive searches possible. In a decision affecting several western states, but subject to review by higher courts, a three-judge panel ruled that a federal law permitting collection of blood samples for DNA analysis from all convicted felons, including those on probation or parole, was unconstitutional. The court in *U.S. v. Kincade* held:

> Although . . . fingerprints do contain unique identifying information, they, like the human voice and the features of the face, are external to the individual. To obtain this identifying information requires no intrusive invasion of bodily privacy. By contrast, while DNA, like fingerprints, identifies an individual, DNA identification results from a forced intrusion into an individual's body. Fingerprinting, involving aspects of an individual's identity routinely exposed to public view, "represents a much less serious intrusion upon personal security than other types of searches and detentions."[22]

The court also noted the greater degree of bodily intrusion involved in collection of DNA samples than in taking fingerprints or mug shots. The law in question specified that blood samples be taken, and the court stressed the very personal nature of the procedure:

> Intrusions into the human body, including the taking of blood, are searches subject to the restrictions of the Fourth Amendment. . . . In virtually every culture around the world, human blood possesses great symbolic power, and its spillage—whether in a drop or in a torrent—has carried enormous cultural significance. Throughout history, we have waged war, organized societies and religions, and created myths based upon the substance.[23]

Most law enforcement agencies collect DNA samples by means of either blood tests or buccal swabs, which are cotton swabs used to take skin cells from the lining of the mouth. Either method, whether plunging a needle below the skin or swabbing inside someone's mouth, involve an intrusion into the body. Newer methods of collecting DNA that could be done without breaking the skin or entering the mouth might become more commonplace, but they will still involve taking a person's cells.

• **Does it matter how police collect DNA samples, or is it always invasive?**

DNA contains extremely private information.

Collecting a DNA sample also takes information that is extremely private. People who have been arrested are required to provide certain information for identification purposes. Booking procedures typically involve taking mug-shot photographs from the front and the profile and inking all of the suspect's fingers to make fingerprint records. However, privacy advocates distinguish this type of information, used for identification purposes, with DNA, which can provide many types of information about an individual. A person's DNA carries many secrets, such as familial relationships and the likelihood of contracting certain diseases such as cancer, heart diseases, and neurological disorders. Scientific advancements occur on a continuous basis, and therefore scientists will likely discover many more secrets that can be concealed by a person's DNA.

Barry Steinhardt, associate director of the American Civil Liberties Union (ACLU), testifying before the National Commission on the Future of DNA Evidence, made a distinction between the collection of fingerprints, which are routinely collected from arrestees, and DNA samples, which are not currently collected during most arrests. He cautioned:

> Drawing a DNA sample is not the same as taking a fingerprint. Fingerprints are two-dimensional representations of the physical attributes of our fingertips. They are useful only as a form of identification. DNA profiling may be used for identification purposes, but the DNA itself represents far more than a fingerprint. Indeed, it trivializes DNA data banking to call it a genetic fingerprint. . . .[24]

Addressing law enforcement officials, attorney Jim Wooley made similar comments about the comparison between a DNA profile and a mug shot: "[A DNA profile is] very different from a mug shot. From a mug shot you can't tell whether or not somebody is going to get sick. There is no theoretical possibility you can abuse that mug shot. . . . The whole world knows what he looks like anyway."[25]

- **If police have unsolved murders to deal with, would they really have time to test for a suspect's likelihood of developing cancer?**

Although proponents of law-enforcement data banks maintain that the DNA profile collected by standard identification testing consists of only a few sites on the DNA that do not contain any information useful to medical research, several privacy advocates have warned that with the rate of advancement in medical research, that could change at any time, and perhaps one of the markers will be linked to some disease. Additionally, most states retain the original blood or saliva sample, which could be reanalyzed for a more complete DNA profile.

Building DNA data banks present opportunities for abuse.

Most civil libertarians are less concerned about the collection and use of DNA evidence in cases where other evidence exists. Under some circumstances, a DNA test would almost automatically be considered reasonable. For example, in a rape case in which DNA evidence could be collected from the victim, and in which there is a suspect to whom all other evidence points, a court would almost certainly order the suspect to submit to a DNA test. However, most jurisdictions require people convicted of rape and other violent crimes to submit a DNA sample, even if they are not suspected of committing any other crimes.

The primary concern of civil libertarians is the growing number of DNA profiles that law enforcement officials are entering into state and federal DNA data banks, which are computerized records that match a person's DNA profile to crime scene evidence. Investigators trying to solve a crime can compare DNA evidence taken from the crime scene to the thousands of personal DNA profiles stored in the data banks. Similarly, a person whose DNA sample is collected for investigation of one crime can be compared to DNA evidence taken from unsolved crimes nationwide.

These DNA data banks collect the genetic profiles of thousands of people and allow access to these profiles to law enforcement officials around the nation. Given the many types of private information encoded in a person's DNA, many people worry that the temptation and opportunity to use DNA data banks for other purposes are too great. University of California sociologist Troy Duster warns that the increasing speed of supercomputers, allowing trillions of calculations per second in interpreting

ACLU Raises Concern About Genetic Discrimination
Testimony of Barry Steinhardt

I understand that the CODIS system only contains a limited amount of genetic information compiled for identification purposes. But the amount of personal and private data contained in a DNA specimen makes its seizure extraordinary in both its nature and scope. The DNA samples that are being held by the federal, state and local governments can provide insights into the most personal family relationships and the most intimate workings of the human body, including the likelihood of the occurrence of thousands of genetic conditions and diseases. DNA may reveal private information such as legitimacy at birth, and there are many who will claim that there are genetic markers for aggression, substance addiction, criminal tendencies and sexual orientation.

And because genetic information pertains not only to the individual whose DNA is sampled, but to everyone who shares in that person's bloodline, potential threats to genetic privacy posed by their collection extend well beyond the millions of people whose samples are currently on file. . . .

Genetic discrimination by the government is not merely an artifact of the distant past. During the 1970s, the Air Force refused to allow healthy individuals who carried one copy of the sickle-cell gene to engage in flight training, even genetic data, might encourage criminologists to once again try to search for racial and ethnic predisposition to crime, a now-discredited approach of nineteenth-century criminologists. At the time, phrenology, or the study of the structure of the skull, was in vogue and thought to offer clues to human behavior. Duster calls the availability of databases and computer analysis a "recurring seduction to false precision" that could fuel misleading stereotypes about minorities and crime.[26]

though two copies of the gene are needed for symptoms of sickle-cell disease to develop. The Lawrence Livermore laboratory only recently settled a case brought by African American employees who were subjected to secret genetic testing for the sickle cell trait.

Genetic discrimination by private industry is becoming increasingly commonplace as well. A 1997 survey conducted by the American Management Association found that six to ten percent of responding employers (well over 6,000 companies) used genetic testing for employment purposes. The Council for Responsible Genetics, a nonprofit advocacy group based in Cambridge, Mass. has documented hundreds of cases in which healthy people have been denied insurance or a job based on genetic "predictions."

In short, there is a frightening potential for a brave new world where genetic information is routinely collected and its use results in abuse and discrimination.

Source: House Judiciary Committe, Subcommittee on Crime, *Legislative hearing on H.R. 2810, the "Violent Offender DNA Identification Act of 1999"; H.R. 3087, the "DNA Backlog Elimination Act"; and H.R. 3375, the "Convicted Offender DNA Index Systems Support Act"* 106th Cong. 2d Sess. (2000).

Duster cautions that as the number of DNA profiles in the databases increases—as is happening rapidly as states increase the number of offenses for which DNA samples are mandated and begin to collect DNA from arrestees and even by canvassing neighborhoods—the likelihood of trying to identify genes that predispose people to commit crimes will also increase. Such a discovery could pose a threat to civil liberties. Mark Rothstein warns that "at [a] parole hearing the government might attempt to show that a genetic predisposition to violence or other antisocial behavior makes the individual likely to be a recidivist who should not be granted parole." [27] Dorothy Nelkin and Lori Andrews believe that the discovery could have a more sweeping impact, suggesting that if "genetic predispositions" to crime can be identified, law enforcement officials might engage in "measures to prevent crime by circumscribing the rights of people thought to have criminal genes. This might include identifying those with antisocial genes, keeping them under surveillance, or preventatively detaining them." [28]

The obvious problem with such practices is that they turn the traditional notion of "innocent until proven guilty" on its head. Duster warns: "[C]orrelation is not causation, and like the phrenology of the nineteenth century, these markers will be precisely that: markers, not explanatory of the causes of violent crime. . . . [A major factor overlooked by such claims] is interaction with the environment at every level." [29]

Summary

Civil libertarians believe that the collection of DNA is a serious invasion of privacy. Unlike fingerprints and mug shots, DNA contains private information, and collecting DNA requires taking a person's living cells. As states expand the collection of DNA to people convicted of a much wider variety of offenses, many people are raising questions about whether the government should be collecting such sensitive information in the absence of any individualized suspicion that someone has done something wrong. These concerns are perhaps even more relevant as states start collecting DNA from people who have been arrested but have not yet been found guilty of any wrongdoing.

DNA Profiling Has the Sole Purpose of Solving Actual Crimes

P roponents of law and order dismiss suggestions that privacy concerns should stem efforts to collect DNA for law enforcement purposes. Using DNA profiles is an important tool for identifying criminals, more important even than fingerprints, because DNA evidence can be recovered in so many ways. The purpose of this evidence is not to find out anything about the person's health or other characteristics, but simply to identify the suspect. A story recounted by Terry Gainer, executive assistant chief of police for the District of Columbia, shows how DNA can be used to identify a suspect, especially in cases in which little traditional evidence exists. During a robbery, the victim and the robber exchanged gunfire, and the victim thought that he had hit the burglar with one of his shots. The victim, however, did not get a good look at the robber, nor was a video camera running, and the robber appeared to have made a clean getaway.

The detectives went to local hospitals to see if anyone had sought treatment for a gunshot wound. As Gainer explained, "Lo and behold, someone walked into the hospital complaining of a through-and-through gunshot wound to the arm. As you might suspect, the story that they gave that detective is the one you've heard a million times, they were walking down the street, heard a noise and suddenly were shot in the arm and knew not where it came from. How many times have we heard a story like that?" [30] Of course, the police had their suspicions, and due to a bit of luck, they were able to make the collar. Gainer said DNA made the arrest possible:

> There was a bullet in the wall, and instead of just traditionally taking that bullet out and sending it down to firearms for it to be tested in the hopes that either IBIS or drug firer or brass catcher could link that baby up, they first sent it to be checked for DNA because the thought was that perhaps the bullet passed through the offender, and that's exactly what had occurred. They linked the offender to that case from the recovered fired bullet in the wall. [31]

Although civil libertarians compare the collection of DNA samples to the big-brother-dominated society of George Orwell's *1984*, many politicians and law enforcement officials dismiss the claims of the ACLU and other civil libertarians. Former New York Mayor Rudolph Giuliani declared, "The opposition to DNA on the theory that this invades privacy—which comes mostly from the ACLU—is no more compelling than the opposition to fingerprinting when it first started." [32] In the opinion of most law enforcement officials, DNA evidence helps solve crimes, and the police are not interested in collecting other types of genetic information. With backlogs of unsolved cases, crime labs do not have the time to analyze whether suspects are likely to develop a disease: They are too busy trying to solve rapes and murders. In the opinion of many people in the law enforcement community, innocent people have nothing to worry about, and the states and federal government should be given broad latitude in collecting DNA samples from people who might be responsible for unsolved or future crimes.

DNA profiles are created for identification purposes only.

Privacy advocates have expressed concern that providing a DNA sample involves surrendering sensitive genetic information such as susceptibility to certain diseases. However, proponents of DNA testing dismiss such claims. Although a person's DNA contains a great deal of information, the DNA profile used in law enforcement does not contain clues to any information other than the sequence of molecules at this particular location. Human DNA contains genes, which help to determine a person's appearance and many other characteristics and constitute about 3 percent of the DNA. The other 97 percent has no known value and is therefore often referred to as junk DNA. Forensic DNA testing relies mostly on junk DNA.

The FBI's CODIS database has selected thirteen core locations for testing, and with the exception of the location that identifies gender, none of them has any particular significance. Like the loops and ridges of a fingerprint, there is no significance to the pattern, other than the fact that it differs from person to person. The reason for including the gender marker is that in investigating rape cases, investigators often need to distinguish between the victim's DNA and the rapist's DNA when analyzing a specimen collected from the crime scene or rape kit.

Not only is DNA an identification method, it is an excellent one that offers the same investigatory powers as fingerprints, but is perhaps more useful due to the variety of evidence that can be retrieved.

• **Is it fair to compare DNA to a fingerprint or mug shot?**

IDENTIFICATION SECTION - POLICE DEPARTMENT

Name: M_ Richard

Alias: none

Photo #: 11? 946 -628   Crim. Record #: 71545   F.P. FORMULA

Prints Taken By: L. Berk   Date: 10-19-94

At: Metro. Pct 3

Classified By:

| 1. RIGHT THUMB | 2. RIGHT INDEX | 3. RIGHT MIDDLE | 4. RIGHT RING | 5. RIGHT LITTLE |
| 6. LEFT THUMB | 7. LEFT INDEX | 8. LEFT MIDDLE | 9. LEFT RING | 10. LEFT LITTLE |

Long before the practice of collecting a sample of an arrestee's DNA was introduced, law enforcement officials required arrestees to complete fingerprint charts. Proponents for compiling DNA profiles in police data banks view DNA samples as no more sacred than the fingerprints police currently acquire.

DNA samples can be collected in a non-invasive manner.

Most challenges to the collection of DNA samples have been based on claims that the collection of DNA constitutes an unreasonable search or seizure in violation of the Fourth Amendment to the U.S. Constitution. Although most courts have upheld laws allowing law enforcement officials widespread power to collect DNA samples, at least one federal court—in a decision affecting the law in several states—has struck down a law requiring parolees to provide blood samples for DNA data banking as an unreasonable search in violation of the Fourth Amendment, which prohibits unreasonable searches and seizures.[33] However, proponents of DNA testing have continued to press for broader collection powers on two grounds. First, that methods of DNA collection other than drawing blood do not constitute a "search or seizure," and second, that even if collecting DNA samples constitutes a search or seizure, that the procedure is a reasonable search or seizure.

While drawing blood for various law enforcement purposes, such as drug or blood-alcohol testing, has long been held to be a type of search or seizure, drawing blood is not the only method available for collecting DNA. For example, police can use a "buccal swab," a cotton swab that can be gently rubbed against the inside of a person's cheek. Because DNA is found in all living cells, the development of new methods of collection is likely to continue. Some advocates of DNA testing believe that methods of collecting DNA samples other than blood tests do not constitute searches for the purpose of implicating Fourth Amendment protections. Attorney Jim Wooley told an audience of law enforcement officials that a method such as using a buccal swab might not constitute a search: "Because it's so easy to get them, you don't have an expectation of privacy, which is the linchpin of Fourth Amendment analysis," he said. He warned investigators, however, that "[people] have an expectation of privacy with respect to . . . genetic material in that setting, and I think whether you take it from a buccal swab or from a [needle], I think you need to justify that under the Fourth Amendment. . . ."[34]

- **Does any method of DNA collection seem less invasive than others?**

Others argue that increasingly non-invasive methods of DNA collection do not constitute searches for purposes of the Fourth Amendment. In a law review article, Ben Quarmby wrote:

> Modern DNA sampling methods no longer violate reasonable societal expectations of privacy. . . . DNA [can be extracted] by applying a sticky patch to the skin on an individual's forearm for a moment to acquire epidermal cells without puncturing the skin [sic] surface. There is no sub-dermal physical intrusion. The invasion of personal space required is minimal. The patch is applied and removed in a matter of seconds. . . . The cell extraction procedure would therefore not constitute a search, and the provisions of the [Fourth] Amendment would not be called into play.[35]

Although having a "sticky patch" attached to the skin is certainly less painful than a needle, and even though the sticky patch would not break the skin, many people would undoubtedly feel violated by having their skin cells collected by law enforcement officials. Therefore, most proponents of aggressively collecting DNA samples from suspects, or potential suspects, are willing to concede that collecting DNA samples does constitute a search or seizure, but maintain that collecting DNA samples is often reasonable, and therefore does not violate the Fourth Amendment.

The security of DNA data banks are assured.

Although privacy advocates fear that DNA data banks will be misused and their security will be compromised, law enforcement officials take security issues seriously. Former U.S. Attorney General Janet Reno, a strong supporter of DNA data banks, warned that their success depended on avoiding situations in which data could be accessed by outsiders or used inappropriately. She said:

> [We] must continue to integrate DNA technology into our criminal justice system in ways that maximizes its investigative

potential, but at the same time done in a way that serves to promote public trust in the system. Our civil rights and civil liberties are precious not only to privacy advocates, but to every single one of us, and as we find new and better ways to solve crimes using this powerful tool we must be mindful of our stewardship of the rights of the individual, the rights of the accused. We must proceed wisely, thoughtfully, and with an eye towards the constitution and how it will be interpreted in light of these new applications of technology.[36]

Paul Ferrara, who oversees Virginia's system of crime laboratories, including its DNA data bank, says that DNA data banks "are the best regulated data banks in the country." He also noted that DNA data banks are not a likely source of samples for health care research, and will not lead to insurance or employment discrimination: "Ironically, [privacy advocates] worry about insurance companies and employers who, of course, as a matter of routine ask for blood samples or urine samples anyway [from] which all of this information could be ascertained."[37]

THE LETTER OF THE LAW

Protections Included in Virginia's Data Bank Law

Any person who, without authority, disseminates information contained in the data bank shall be guilty of a Class 3 misdemeanor. Any person who disseminates, receives, or otherwise uses or attempts to so use information in the data bank, knowing that such dissemination, receipt, or use is for a purpose other than as authorized by law, shall be guilty of a Class 1 misdemeanor.

Except as authorized by law, any person who, for purposes of having DNA analysis performed, obtains or attempts to obtain any sample submitted to the Division of Forensic Science for analysis shall be guilty of a Class 5 felony.

Source: Va. Code § 19.2–310.6 (2004).

Attorney Jim Wooley dismisses the idea that law enforcement officials would have any interest in using DNA samples to search for predisposition to disease. He explained to a group of law enforcement officers that they would probably hear such criticisms:

[People bring up the] theoretical possibility of things that could be done with DNA other than match it, use it for crime solving purposes. [However,] the argument that I know to be true and solid at this point is no cop in his right mind is going to give a rat's [tail] about a disease gene and nobody is going to be motivated to do anything with that capability, and it is purely a theoretical thing.[38]

- **How can misuse of DNA data banks be monitored?**

Summary

Law enforcement officials and law-and-order politicians believe that the usefulness of collecting DNA samples far outweighs any privacy concerns. Law enforcement officials say that DNA profiling is a method of establishing identity and nothing else. It is too useful a tool to let theoretical fears of misuse interfere with its availability to investigators.

DNA Banks Are Growing Too Rapidly

I n late 2002 and early 2003, police in Baton Rouge, Louisiana, were intensifying their search for a serial killer who was preying on local women. The killings had caused widespread fear because it seemed impossible to predict who would be next: The victims varied both in age and race, a rarity in serial killings. With public hysteria at a fevered pitch, an anonymous tip line was drawing calls that provided a lot of dead ends. Nevertheless, police investigated the leads, no matter how vague, in an attempt to stop the killings.

The police mounted what is known as a DNA dragnet, a widespread collection of DNA samples from people who meet a general description or a suspected profile. For example, police might try to collect samples from short African-American men, from shy white men, or even from every man in a small town. Often, people who drive certain types of vehicles are targeted. In

Baton Rouge, police were on the lookout for a man driving a white pickup truck, and they collected more than one thousand DNA samples from area men using buccal swabs to take cells from the linings of their cheeks. Generally, police need to have some sort of reason to collect DNA evidence from people, so these dragnets are conducted on what police say is a voluntary basis—people are essentially offered a chance to "clear their names." However, two problems immediately stand out. First, the people tested often have no reason to be suspected, and therefore have no suspicion to clear up. Second, by refusing a test, a person immediately draws the attention of police.

> • **Should an innocent person have the right to refuse a DNA test? Should the police be allowed to focus their investigation on people who refuse DNA tests?**

When officers called upon Shannon Kohler, a welder, and asked him for a DNA sample, he refused. They had sought him out in response to an anonymous tip, but there was no evidence linking him to the case, other than the extremely weak connection that he had once worked at a business on the same street where one victim's cell phone was found. He denied any involvement in the killings and offered phone records to show that he was home when the murders were committed. He refused, however, to let officers take a DNA sample. In response, law enforcement officials obtained a court order compelling Kohler to submit to a DNA test.

He complied with the order, and the test confirmed what he had been saying—that he was not the killer. Now, however, the police had a sample of his DNA, and all of the genetic information that it carries with it. Additionally, the proceedings were made public, and his name ended up in the newspapers and television. The police caught the real killer, but they held on to the DNA samples and the profiles that were generated from the samples. In June 2003, Kohler filed a lawsuit in federal court seeking the return of his DNA.

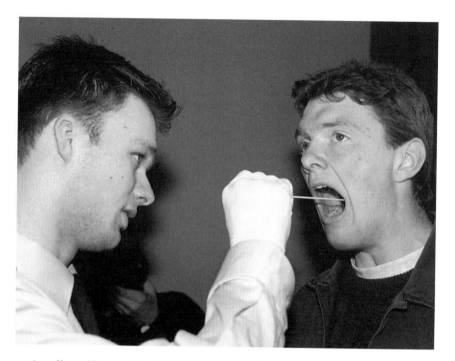

A police officer collects DNA from a man by using a buccal swab to lift cells from the lining of his inner cheek as part of a DNA dragnet. Law enforcement officials employ such dragnets to allow people who generally fit the profile of a suspected criminal to come forward and clear their names. Civil libertarians are against such mass DNA collections, arguing that this practice does not meet the criterion of individualized suspicion.

Civil libertarians, who are extremely concerned about the implications of huge genetic databases being built by the government, believe that law enforcement officials are going too far in collecting DNA samples. They have been fighting a losing battle against laws that allow the collection of DNA from all convicted felons, but they are redoubling efforts to prevent police officers from collecting DNA samples from people who have been arrested but not convicted, and they are staunchly against the type of DNA dragnet conducted in Baton Rouge.

Collection of DNA from all convicted felons is not based on individualized suspicion.

When states began to enact DNA collection laws, civil libertarians, including groups such as the ACLU, raised concerns about the privacy of individuals and the rights of the accused. Originally, DNA was collected only from people who had been convicted of especially violent crimes, and ones in which crime scene DNA evidence was likely to be relevant, such as rape or murder. The justification for these laws was threefold. First, there was a high likelihood that a convicted rapist or murderer had in fact committed other crimes, based on what the justice system knew about recidivism rates—rates of repeat offenses. Second, because of the violent nature of the crimes, DNA evidence such as blood or semen was likely to have been left at the scene of the crime, and crime scene investigators were likely to have collected evidence that could contain the perpetrator's DNA. Third, the serious nature of the offenses increased the need for preventing and solving such crimes.

Not long, however, after states began to mandate the collection of DNA from convicted rapists and murderers, they began to expand their collection processes to include the collection of DNA from people convicted of other types of felonies, such as carjacking and armed robbery. Many included so-called property crimes, in which no person was physically harmed; the most common example was burglary. Recently, many states have expanded their DNA collection laws to include all felonies, as well as juvenile offenses that would be considered felonies in the adult criminal courts. The ACLU opposed the expansion of DNA collection from convicted felons, which associate director Barry Steinhardt called "intrusive, unreasonable searches made without the individualized suspicion required by the Fourth Amendment and analogous provisions of state constitutions."[39]

The term individualized suspicion refers to the justification that the Supreme Court has typically required for searches conducted without a search warrant. The framers of the Constitution

enacted the Fourth Amendment as a reaction to previous practices under British rule, in which the government could look for
evidence against anyone in order to bring charges against the
person. As Justice Day noted in *Weeks* v. *U.S.*:

> [The Fourth Amendment] took its origin in . . . securing to the
> American people, among other things, those safeguards which
> had grown up in England to protect the people from unreason-
> able searches and seizures, such as were permitted under the
> general warrants issued under authority of the government, by
> which there had been invasions of the home and privacy of the

FROM THE BENCH

Supreme Court Requires "Individualized Suspicion" for Law Enforcement Searches

In *Martinez-Fuerte*, we entertained Fourth Amendment challenges to stops at two permanent immigration checkpoints located on major United States highways less than 100 miles from the Mexican border. We noted at the outset the particular context in which the constitutional question arose, describing in some detail the "formidable law enforcement problems" posed by the northbound tide of illegal entrants into the United States. . . .

In so finding, we emphasized the difficulty of effectively containing illegal immigration at the border itself. . . . We also stressed the impracticality of the particularized study of a given car to discern whether it was transporting illegal aliens, as well as the relatively modest degree of intrusion entailed by the stops. . . .

In *Sitz*, we evaluated the constitutionality of a Michigan highway sobriety checkpoint program. The *Sitz* checkpoint involved brief suspicionless stops of motorists so that police officers could detect signs of intoxication and remove impaired drivers from the road. . . . Motorists who exhibited signs of intoxication were diverted for a license and registration check and, if warranted, further sobriety tests. . . . This checkpoint program was clearly aimed at reducing the immediate hazard posed by the presence of drunk drivers on the highways, and there was an obvious connection between the imperative of highway safety and the law enforcement practice at issue. The gravity of the drunk driving problem and the magnitude of the State's interest in getting drunk drivers off the road weighed heavily in our determination that the program was constitutional. . . .

citizens, and the seizure of their private papers in support of charges, real or imaginary, [made] against them. Such practices had also received sanction under warrants and seizures under the so-called writs of assistance, issued in the American colonies. . . . Resistance to these practices had established the principle which was enacted into the fundamental law in the [Fourth] Amendment, that a man's house was his castle, and not to be invaded by any general authority to search and seize his goods and papers.[40]

Although the Supreme Court has throughout the years carved out many exceptions to the general requirement that

In *Prouse*, we invalidated a discretionary, suspicionless stop for a spot check of a motorist's driver's license and vehicle registration. The officer's conduct in that case was unconstitutional primarily on account of his exercise of "standardless and unconstrained discretion." . . . We nonetheless acknowledged the States' "vital interest in ensuring that only those qualified to do so are permitted to operate motor vehicles, that these vehicles are fit for safe operation, and hence that licensing, registration, and vehicle inspection requirements are being observed." . . . Accordingly, we suggested that "[q]uestioning of all oncoming traffic at roadblock-type stops" would be a lawful means of serving this interest in highway safety. . . .

We have never approved a checkpoint program whose primary purpose was to detect evidence of ordinary criminal wrongdoing. Rather, our checkpoint cases have recognized only limited exceptions to the general rule that a seizure must be accompanied by some measure of individualized suspicion. We suggested in *Prouse* that we would not credit the "general interest in crime control" as justification for a regime of suspicionless stops. . . . Consistent with this suggestion, each of the checkpoint programs that we have approved was designed primarily to serve purposes closely related to the problems of policing the border or the necessity of ensuring roadway safety. Because the primary purpose of the Indianapolis narcotics checkpoint program is to uncover evidence of ordinary criminal wrongdoing, the program contravenes the Fourth Amendment.

Source: *City of Indianapolis v. Edmond*, 531 U.S. 32 (2000)

searches cannot be conducted without a warrant, such as allowing police to frisk a person suspected of carrying a weapon, the
Court has generally maintained a requirement that the person
conducting the search must have some sort of individualized
suspicion justifying the search. Otherwise, the government would
have the same type of power to conduct general searches of the
citizenry that the framers of the Constitution so frowned upon.
For example, in *City of Indianapolis* v. *Edmond,* the Court forbade
the practice of randomly stopping cars to search for drugs,
noting: "We decline to suspend the usual requirement of individualized suspicion where the police seek to employ a checkpoint
primarily for the ordinary enterprise of investigating crimes. We
cannot sanction stops justified only by the generalized and ever-
present possibility that interrogation and inspection may reveal
that any given motorist has committed some crime." [41]

The ACLU and other civil libertarians believe that the collection of DNA samples from all convicted felons is dangerously
similar to stopping cars randomly to search for drugs. Both are
designed to detect evidence of crime, and both are done without
any particular hunch that the individual being searched has done
anything wrong. While it might be true that convicted felons have
committed a crime in the past, there is no real reason to suspect
that they will do so in the future. Law enforcement officials might
have a strong case that rapists are likely to commit multiple
crimes and leave DNA evidence at crime scenes; however, there is
much less reason to believe that someone who has been convicted
of burglary is going to commit a crime in which DNA evidence
will be collected at the crime scene.

The lack of individualized suspicion inherent in collecting
DNA samples from all convicted felons was central to the controversial *U.S.* v. *Kincade* ruling. Rejecting the argument that
past convictions justified future searches, the court stated:

> The government suggests [that two past Supreme Court cases
> regarding individualized suspicion] do not apply to searches

pursuant to the Act, because both Supreme Court cases dealt with programs affecting "law abiding citizens," while the Act addresses "probationers and felons." . . . [A] program of suspicionless searches, *conducted for law enforcement purposes*, violates the Fourth Amendment, whether the person searched is a model citizen (and thus the search will produce no useful evidence), or whether he is not law-abiding (and as a result evidence of a crime may sometimes be obtained). Indeed, it would be a unique construction of the Constitution to hold that Fourth Amendment protections exist only for the benefit of the innocent, and not for all persons in our society, regardless of one's propensity to engage in criminal activity.[42]

- **If police *are* allowed to search prisoners and parolees for drugs at any time, why should they not also be able to collect their DNA?**

Although courts have ruled that people who are currently in jail or prison have lessened privacy rights, these decisions have been based on the need of jailers to maintain safety and control, not on the basis that loss of privacy is part of the punishment for having committed a crime. The *Kincade* court noted this distinction:

[The] purpose of obtaining DNA samples is to obtain material for future use in a permanent DNA data bank to help solve future crimes, no matter how long after the end of the parole term they may be committed. . . . [The purpose of the law,] according to the government, is to further "the overwhelming public interest in creating a comprehensive nationwide DNA bank that will improve the accuracy of criminal prosecutions" for generations to come. It is undoubtedly true that, were we to maintain DNA files on all persons living in this country, we would even more effectively further the public interest in having efficient and orderly criminal prosecutions, just as we would were we willing to sacrifice *all* of our interests in privacy and personal liberty. We chose, however, not to follow that course when we adopted the Fourth Amendment.[43]

Like the judge who wrote the *Kincade* opinion, many people worry that allowing the government to define groups of people who are unworthy of Fourth Amendment protections for the rest of their lives sets a dangerous precedent, because these limits could be extended to other groups. Boston defense attorney Benjamin Keehn argued on *NewsHour with Jim Lehrer* that by effectively saying to convicted felons, "you may be a danger in the future because you were in the past, and therefore we need to register your DNA," the government is assuming ominous new powers. "That is a fundamentally different way that government has heretofore been permitted to treat its citizens," he said. Although statistical evidence suggests that many convicted rapists commit multiple offenses, evidence also suggests that many other groups of people are more likely to commit certain crimes. He worries about a society in which the government is able to make broad assumptions rather than investigating crimes based upon individualized suspicion, wondering aloud, "If we are going to take DNA from prisoners because they are at risk, why shouldn't we take DNA from teenagers, from homeless people, from Catholic priests, from any subgroup of society that some-one is able to make a statistical argument of being at risk?"[44]

Collection of DNA from arrestees violates the principle of "innocent until proven guilty."

Keehn's point is that by removing the requirement of individualized suspicion for the collection of DNA samples, society is sliding down a "slippery slope," meaning that once rules are broken for one group, justifications are frequently made for breaking them for others. Many people share Keehn's concern, and even worry that the United States is moving toward mandatory DNA testing for all of its citizens. Christine Rosen, a fellow at the Ethics and Public Policy Center in Washington,

D.C., warns of a future similar to that portrayed in the movie *Gattaca*, in which a universal DNA data bank determines people's job prospects and other facets of their lives. She wrote:

> In the beginning, the reasons for such databases will be familiar, modern, liberal, and compelling: to cure disease, to catch criminals, to ensure that children have a healthy beginning to their lives. But the end in sight is a drastically different society and way of life. . . . [Our] public and private institutions may know so much about us that equal treatment and personal liberty may become impossible.[45]

Although widespread support for universal DNA collection does not yet exist, privacy advocates warn that American society is indeed headed in that direction. Testifying before the National Commission on the Future of DNA Evidence, the ACLU's Steinhardt pointed out that several states have proposed keeping DNA data obtained in routine screening of newborn babies for inherited diseases, and the military maintains a data bank of the DNA of all military personnel. The most immediate threat, however, to collecting DNA samples from innocent people in order to link them to past or future crimes might be the growing trend to collect DNA samples from all people who are arrested. Steinhardt testified:

> Arrest does not equal guilt and you shouldn't suffer the consequences of guilt until after you have been convicted. . . . A study released by the California state Assembly's Commission on the Status of African-American Males in the early 1990s revealed that 64 percent of the drug arrests of whites and 81 percent of Latinos were not sustainable, and that an astonishing 92 percent of black men arrested by police on drug charges were subsequently released for lack of evidence or inadmissible evidence.[46]

The statistics he cited clearly indicate that a large number of people who are arrested are never convicted, and therefore none of the rationales commonly cited to justify collecting DNA samples from convicted offenders would apply to a large number of arrestees. Added to the insult of being arrested without justification, a person has his or her DNA collected and compared to unsolved crimes while waiting for charges that might never come. This brings us perilously close to a society in which police can round people up, book them on vague charges, and then collect their DNA in the hope—however unlikely—that it matches an unsolved crime. Collecting DNA samples from arrestees therefore encourages false arrests, detention, and searches of innocent people with the goal of finding incriminating evidence, and it also has the danger of having a disproportionate impact on minorities.

In 2003, Virginia began collecting DNA samples from everyone arrested on felony charges and entering DNA profiles developed from these samples into the state's DNA data bank. Although the law provides that the samples and the profiles will be destroyed if the charges are dismissed or the arrestee is found not guilty at trial, a considerable amount of time can pass between arrest and trial. During that time, law enforcement officials can compare the arrestee's DNA profile to DNA taken from unsolved crimes. Therefore, people arrested by police—even those falsely arrested by police—are subjected to intense scrutiny without a reason to link them to any other crime. The potential for abuse led the legal director of the state's ACLU chapter to lament, "Virginia has become a national leader in invading people's privacy."[47]

Law professor Paul Butler warned the government-appointed National Commission on the Future of DNA Evidence that collecting DNA samples from arrestees will have a disparate impact on minorities, especially if people arrested on drug offenses are required to provide samples. He explained:

> [Because, according to Department of Justice statistics,] African Americans are only 13 percent of people who are using drugs, possessing drugs, but they're 75% of the people incarcerated for that, there are a whole lot of people out there

who are not African American who are not being treated by the criminal justice system because the police are focused on African Americans. . . . In California two-thirds of black and Hispanic men are arrested before they reach the age of 30. In the District of Columbia about 50% of young black men are under criminal justice supervision, that is, awaiting trial, probation, or parole or in prison. A lot of the reason for this, the explanation for that disparity is this race based profiling.[48]

Butler's message is ominous: As jurisdictions begin to collect DNA samples from arrestees, American society faces a future in which a significant percentage of Hispanic- and African-American men, and a much smaller percentage of the general population, have their DNA profiles stored in a nationwide database of information that can be used to link them to crimes.

"DNA Dragnets" invade everyone's privacy.

While civil libertarians are not at all pleased with the collection of DNA samples from arrestees, at the very least, arrestees are somewhat protected by the requirement that police must show "probable cause" in order to make an arrest and have a suspect held. Although it is a much lower requirement than proof of guilt beyond a reasonable doubt, which is required for a criminal conviction, police cannot pick people completely at random to have them arrested. Yet, police are beginning to pick people almost completely at random to ask them for DNA samples. So-called "DNA dragnets" have been used for many years in the United Kingdom, and police in the United States, when faced with a series of crimes with no leads, are beginning to ask people meeting a general description to provide DNA samples. Often, these dragnets focus on people of a particular race, if there is any information identifying the race of a potential suspect.

Although law enforcement officials claim that the innocent have nothing to fear in participating in these dragnets, experience suggests that innocent people can suffer a great deal of harm when the government misuses genetic information. Testifying before the Judiciary Committee of the U.S. House of Representatives, attorney Peter Neufeld told a story that should give even innocent people cause for alarm:

> [The] city of Miami was searching for a serial rapist whose DNA links him to assaults on at least six women. As part of the investigation, police have taken more than one-hundred twenty samples from "volunteers" who either resemble the description of the serial rapist or have been the subjects of a tip police received. As part of the search, investigators stopped Jorge Garcia on June 14 of this year because he resembled the description of the perpetrator. Mr. Garcia voluntarily gave a DNA sample which did not match the profile of the rapist.
>
> But instead of destroying the sample once Mr. Garcia was excluded, the crime lab ran it through the State DNA data-bank. To Mr. Garcia's surprise, there was a cold hit—his profile matched that of a profile extracted from evidence collected from the victim of an unrelated 1996 rape. Garcia was arrested and charged with rape. Officials cited it as an example of how DNA data banks help authorities catch rapists. "Had we not had this massive search for this other offender," according to the executive assistant to the Police Chief, "we wouldn't have gotten this guy."
>
> The day after Mr. Garcia's arrest, the victim of the 1996 rape came forward to proclaim Mr. Garcia's innocence. She explained that she and Mr. Garcia had been involved in a long-term relationship, and that the crime lab found his DNA because the couple had consensual sex shortly before she was raped by a stranger. Three days after his arrest, the police dismissed the charges against Mr. Garcia and released him from jail. But what would have happened to Mr. Garcia had the victim died or become incompetent in the intervening years? The price to clear your name shouldn't be surrendering your personal biological information to the government for any and all purposes.[49]

Although he was completely innocent, Garcia spent several days in jail. But that might have been the least of his worries. Undoubtedly, he suffered a great deal of embarrassment when he was arrested, and friends, family, and people in the community were told that he was a suspected rapist. Against his will, details of his past sex life became public knowledge. In the information age, he suffered from a new peril: Six months after the incident, the story of his arrest, but not of his release, remained on the website *sexcriminals.com*.

> • **Would you be comfortable knowing that the police had a sample of your DNA?**

Comparing DNA profiles against unsolved crime databases, with no other reason to suspect a person has committed a crime, make stories like Garcia's more likely in the future, and the results might be even worse. Neufeld raised the point that the victim in the case could have been dead or incompetent to testify. Perhaps even more troubling, the victim in a similar case might not be willing to come forward to exonerate the innocently accused man because they had had an unhappy breakup. Or perhaps the victim would be unwilling to disclose a consensual sexual relationship for fear of embarrassment or angering others.

Summary

Civil libertarians worry that genetic databases are replacing traditional law enforcement methods, which require some measure of suspicion before a person can be investigated. Prisoners, arrestees, and even ordinary citizens are having their genetic profiles entered into electronic databases, even when there is no reason to suspect them of any unsolved crimes.

Comprehensive DNA Data Banks Are Necessary for Law Enforcement

In early 2001, David James McIntosh was in Folsom State Prison in California, serving time for a parole violation because he had failed to register as a convicted sex offender in the community in which he lived. McIntosh was looking forward to being released in about a month, but then something happened that would keep him behind bars for a lot longer. California law requires convicted felons to provide a DNA sample so that their profiles can be entered into the state's DNA data bank. McIntosh's sample was taken while he was locked up at Folsom. On January 29, workers at the state crime lab were comparing DNA profiles from unsolved crimes to new profiles in the database and came up with what law enforcement officials call a "cold hit."

When a thirteen-year-old girl had been raped and murdered in 1984, police were not yet using DNA technology to solve crimes, but in 1999, scientists had been able to develop the killer's DNA profile from the evidence retained from the case. At the time, the profile had not matched any of the profiles in the database, but after McIntosh's profile was added, police finally solved the case by matching crime scene evidence to McIntosh's profile in January 2001. In August 2003, McIntosh was convicted of the rape and murder, based largely on the DNA evidence. Had the state's DNA data bank not linked McIntosh to the crime, he would have been a free man, but the justice system made sure that he did not have the opportunity to rape and kill again.

Although civil libertarians, including groups such as the ACLU, believe that law enforcement officials are too aggressive in collecting DNA samples from too many people, many legislators disagree. Law enforcement officials in some states have successfully lobbied for greater leeway in collecting DNA samples from people who have been arrested, but not convicted; from parolees; from juvenile offenders; and from people convicted of nonviolent crimes. Elsewhere, law enforcement officials continue to press for greater powers in collecting DNA samples because they believe that anyone in the criminal justice system is a potential suspect for unsolved or future crimes.

The need for DNA samples from convicted offenders trumps their privacy interests.

In jurisdictions around the nation, convicted felons have challenged state and federal laws requiring people convicted of certain felonies—or, under some laws, all felonies—but almost every court hearing such challenges has rejected them. Many civil libertarians have criticized the laws on the grounds that they collect evidence without any "individualized suspicion," but courts have agreed with law enforcement officials that the need for DNA generally trumps convicted offenders' privacy interests.

- **Should people who have been convicted of a crime forfeit their right to privacy? For how long?**

People who are convicted of crimes lose many (but not all) of their rights; however, because DNA testing holds so much potential for law enforcement, courts have generally been willing to allow forced blood tests for people convicted of felonies. For example, a Nevada court upheld a law compelling people convicted of certain felonies to provide DNA samples. Rejecting a prisoner's appeal, the court held:

> [The] first consideration to be balanced against the State's interest in the search and seizure at issue is the individual's expectation of privacy. Many jurisdictions have recognized that a convicted person loses some rights to personal privacy that would otherwise be protected under the Fourth Amendment. . . . Another factor balanced against the government's interest is the intrusive nature of the search. Courts considering Fourth Amendment challenges have determined that blood draws from convicted persons to gather genetic information for identification involve only a minimal intrusion.[50]

One might ask why someone who has already been convicted of a crime would need to provide a DNA sample. Law enforcement officials point to the high recidivism rate among rapists, meaning that many rapists rape again and again, committing multiple offenses over time. According to David Coffman, a crime laboratory analyst supervisor for the state of Florida, rapists start at a young age and have numerous victims: "The mean age of the first offense is about 18 years. The number of detected sexual assaults per rapist in prison they've found to be about three. Undetected sexual assaults is about five." Entering a convicted rapist's DNA profile into a data bank deters him from committing another rape after he is released, and identifies him easily if he does commit another rape. "Let's assume that an [average] offender commits eight rapes. Our [data bank] stops him midway through his career, if you want to call it that, thus preventing four rapes," Coffman said.[51]

Additionally, because of the high recidivism rate among rapists, collecting a DNA sample from a convicted rapist is quite likely to help police solve a cold case, by matching the convicted rapist's DNA to an unsolved crime. Some rapists are very likely to have committed rapes before the ones for which they were convicted, and others might have even committed rapes after the ones for which they were convicted. Speaking to law enforcement officials in 2000, Assistant U.S. Attorney General Mary Lou Leary recounted a case in Florida in which a persistent detective

FROM THE BENCH

Federal Court Upholds DNA Testing as Proof of Identity

In arguing against the constitutionality of the Wisconsin law, the plaintiffs rely heavily on *City of Indianapolis* v. *Edmond*. . . . They insist that . . . [DNA collection statutes] can no longer be viewed as reasonable under the Fourth Amendment if their primary purpose is law enforcement. We disagree.

In *City of Indianapolis* v. *Edmond*, the city instituted a motor vehicle checkpoint program whose primary purpose was interdicting illegal narcotics trafficking. The program allowed police to randomly stop motorists on public highways without a warrant and without probably cause. While checking the motorists for compliance with license and registration requirements (as well as intoxication), police used a drug-sniffing dog in hopes of finding evidence of narcotics possession on the driver or in the car.

An important distinction between our case and *Edmond* is that the primary purpose of the Indianapolis checkpoint program was to see if a driver was then and there engaged in illegal drug activity. The primary purpose of the Wisconsin DNA law, on the other hand, is not to search for "evidence" of criminal wrongdoing. Its purpose is to obtain reliable proof of a felon's identity. *Edmond* says much about indiscriminate motor vehicle roadblocks and checkpoints but nothing about safe, nondiscriminatory collection of DNA samples from lawfully incarcerated felons. . . .

Wisconsin's DNA collection statute is, we think, narrowly drawn, and it serves an important state interest. Those inmates subject to testing because they are in custody, are already "seized," and given that DNA is the most reliable evidence of identification—stronger even than fingerprints or photographs, we saw no Fourth Amendment impediment to collecting DNA samples from them pursuant to the Wisconsin law.

Source: *Green* v. *Berge*, No. 01-4080 (7th Cir., Jan. 9, 2004)

investigating a cold case found that the DNA profile matched that of someone already convicted of a rape that had occurred six weeks after the one that he was investigating.[52] By linking a convicted rapist to additional crimes, prosecutors can ensure that a dangerous criminal spends more time behind bars, and solving cold cases also offers peace of mind to rape victims.

Although some people have objected to collecting DNA samples from people on parole or probation because they have already "paid their debt to society," law enforcement officials believe that the same reasons for testing currently incarcerated offenders hold true. National Institute of Justice director Sarah Hart, testifying before Congress, gave the example of a DNA sample taken from a man on parole since 1976, which linked him to an unsolved 1977 murder.[53]

Collecting DNA from criminals, even people not convicted of a violent crime, helps to prevent or solve future violent crimes.

In the *Nevada* case, the person challenging his mandatory DNA sample was not a convicted rapist, but had been convicted of burglary. However, the court rejected his argument that he should not be required to provide a DNA sample because he had not been convicted of a violent crime. Many states collect DNA samples from nonviolent offenders, and law enforcement officials maintain that there is ample reason to do so.

Dr. Paul Ferrara, director of the Virginia Forensics Division, believes that Virginia has benefited enormously from taking DNA samples from nonviolent offenders. When the state first began to keep a database of DNA samples in 1989, only people convicted of violent crimes such as rape and murder were tested. In the following year, however, collection was expanded to include all convicted felons. Speaking in 2000, Dr. Ferrara told an audience of law enforcement officials, "If our DNA data bank was [limited], as it was in 1989, for that one year, the hit rate would be . . . half of what it is today."[54] To that date, the state's

DNA data bank had helped to solve 183 crimes, and by the end of 2002, it had helped to solve more than one thousand.

- **Is there a difference in keeping a large database of finger-prints and keeping a large database of DNA profiles?**

Dr. Ferrara dismissed claims that collecting DNA samples from nonviolent offenders is not worthwhile:

> I'll tell you this, 49 of those [183] persons that we identified . . . were in our data bank because of property crimes. . . . For those of you who have heard, *Oh, what are you taking samples from check cutters and paper hangers for?* . . . Seven had convictions for uttering and forgery. . . . [Some people say that a] drug user is not . . . going to be committing future violent crimes. Well, 18 of . . . the people were in there for drug possession/distribution charges.[55]

Florida joined Virginia among the first states to establish DNA data banks, but Florida broadened the scope of DNA collection more slowly. Law enforcement officials in that state made a concerted effort to persuade the legislature to collect samples from people convicted of burglary. Their efforts were buoyed by statistics from the state's DNA data bank. Among violent crimes solved with the help of the DNA data bank, many offenders had previous convictions for burglary and other crimes. According to David Coffman, a crime laboratory analyst supervisor for the state of Florida, a vast majority of people convicted of rape and homicide also had convictions for other crimes:

> Eleven percent had a previous firearm possession. Thirty percent had a previous drug charge. Thirty-four percent had a previous grand theft. Thirty-four percent had a previous robbery. Fifty-two percent had a burglary, and only 18 percent of the people we linked to rape and homicide had only the crimes that we collect for in their criminal history.[56]

In other words, among the rapes and murders solved through the use of the DNA data bank in Florida, 82 percent of the offenders had also been convicted of crimes for which DNA samples were, at the time, not collected upon conviction. Although these particular people were included because they had also committed crimes for which DNA samples are collected, the implication is that some of the many unsolved crimes might have been convicted by other people with prior convictions that did not require collecting a DNA sample.

While Florida was considering the proposal to require collecting a DNA sample upon conviction for burglary, the ACLU and other civil libertarians challenged the proposal, saying that there was not enough evidence that people who committed burglaries were likely to commit violent crimes in the future. Coffman, however, found that the numbers of violent acts were similar among all people who had been convicted of burglary:

> I was criticized by a national organization, ACLU, for maybe not having a broad enough database of information. I had a couple hundred cases to look at.
>
> So I went to our prisons, and I said, Would you mind looking at the approximately 200,000 people that are either on probation or in our prisons . . . Fourteen percent of [people in prison or on probation for burglary] had a prior . . . homicide. . . . Nine percent had sexual assault. Thirteen percent had aggravated battery [which frequently can be a sex offense] Nine percent with lewd acts with a 45 percent total. . . .
>
> So 45 to 52, that's a statistically valid comparison, and it was a much larger sampling that we took it from. So we feel very justified in adding burglary to our database to help solve crimes.[57]

Plea bargaining provides another reason for broadening the scope of offenses for which conviction requires the collection of DNA samples. In the plea-bargaining process, a person accused of a crime enters a guilty plea in exchange for a lighter punishment.

Prosecutors often use this tactic when they feel a conviction might be difficult, but criminal defendants accept plea bargains in order to avoid the risk of more serious punishment. Frequently, plea bargaining involves pleading guilty to a less serious crime than the one with which the defendant was originally charged. For example, a person charged with murder might plead guilty to manslaughter, which carries a lighter sentence.

The main goal of DNA data banking is to prevent or solve serious crimes, and because people who commit serious crimes often plead guilty to less serious charges, Coffman believes that people convicted of certain so-called less serious crimes should also have their DNA added to data banks. Responding to inquiries about why certain suspects had not been included in the state's data bank, even though they had been charged with sexual assault, he discovered that many people had been charged with sexual assault but had pleaded guilty to other crimes. He then spoke with prosecutors around the state and learned that a common plea among people charged with sexual assault was the lesser charge of aggravated battery. The state later added aggravated battery to the list of offenses in its DNA data bank law.

Coffman also believes that people convicted of crimes but on release via parole or probation should be subject to DNA testing. He cited statistics indicating that among 300,000 people on community supervision, "13,200 people were murdered by those people; 13,000 people were raped by those 300,000; 39,500 were robbed; 39,600 were burglarized; 19,200 were assaulted and 7,900 stole a car," warning "these people are out on the street and they're committing these crimes."[58]

A more controversial position has been to collect DNA samples from juvenile offenders. Although their juvenile records typically would be expunged when they reached a certain age—a tradition offering many juvenile offenders another chance at leading a successful life—their DNA samples would remain in a data bank and available to law enforcement officers. Ferrara considers samples from juvenile offenders to be an important part of Virginia's DNA data bank: "Not all juveniles are going to become adult criminals, but for the few who are, the sooner we have them in the system the better," he told *USA Today.*[59]

Collecting DNA samples upon arrest aids law enforcement.

The Virginia legislature created further controversy by expanding its DNA collection law to mandate collection of samples from anyone *arrested* for a violent felony. Despite criticism by groups such as the ACLU, local law enforcement officials praised the law, noting that it would help them to quickly identify criminals who move from place to place. This was a special concern in the wake of the well-publicized sniper attacks in Virginia, Maryland, and the District of Columbia.

> • **How quickly should an arrestee's DNA results be processed? Should his or her results be compared to unsolved crimes, or should this be done only after a conviction?**

Law enforcement officials have long supported the expansion of DNA collection to include people arrested for crimes. During his 2000 State of the City address, former New York Mayor Rudolph Giuliani noted how useful the collection of DNA from arrestees can be. He noted:

> Last year, the Police arrested a man named Ahron Kee for larceny. He was also suspected of rape. When the Police got Ahron Kee into the Precinct and questioned him on the larceny charge, they gave him a cup of coffee. He drank the coffee. The Police went and booked him for the larceny, and they took the cup. They got his DNA from his saliva. And they matched his DNA to the DNA of a man who committed three murders and three rapes. Ahron Kee is now in the process of being prosecuted for all of those crimes. This illustrates DNA's potential for making us much more effective in catching criminals and reducing crime, particularly crimes of rape and sexual assault.[60]

Rather than requiring police to resort to such trickery, Giuliani said, "[We] should ultimately take DNA from anybody that we take a fingerprint from."[61]

Comprehensive DNA data banks pose no threat to the innocent.

Some people have even gone so far as to say that DNA samples should be taken from everyone, whether or not they have had any reason to be suspected of doing anything wrong. In arguing for building a comprehensive database including the DNA profiles of everyone living in the nation, advocates of such a proposal have pointed out that it would eliminate the racial bias inherent in building databases of arrestees' profiles, because members of minority groups are arrested more often than whites.

Additionally, a group of law professors wrote that a database of every person's DNA would have many advantages: "Speedier apprehension would halt crime sprees. Potential lawbreakers may avoid crimes because they know their DNA profiles will routinely be compared to crime scene evidence. More efficient investigations would free police resources."[62] Although some people are concerned about the civil liberty implications of such a system, supporters counter that innocent people would not have to worry and, in fact, would be more likely to be acquitted when falsely accused.

Summary

Civil libertarians say that building databases of DNA profiles poses threats to ordinary citizens, but law enforcement officials disagree, saying that the more people who are included in DNA data banks, the more crimes that can be prevented or solved. Already, states collect DNA from most convicted felons, and a new trend is to require testing of arrestees. Some people have even called for a universal database, saying that the innocent have nothing to fear.

The Most Pressing Use for DNA Evidence Is Freeing the Wrongly Convicted

K irk Bloodsworth today stands as a symbol of the power of DNA evidence as a tool for exonerating the innocent. Convicted of murder in 1985 and sentenced to death, Bloodsworth received a pardon from the governor of Maryland in 1993. In September 2003, police charged another man with the murder for which Bloodsworth had been convicted.

The crime was the type of horrific incident that causes great public alarm, putting increased pressure on police to apprehend a suspect and on district attorneys to convict that suspect. A nine-year-old girl was raped and murdered, beaten to death with a rock. An anonymous caller claimed to have seen Bloodsworth with the young victim before the murder, and after his arrest, several people testified that they too had seen Bloodsworth with the victim. Additionally, Bloodsworth had told people on the day of the murder that he had done "something terrible" that would jeopardize his marriage. Police testified that during the interrogation, Bloodsworth had mentioned a "bloody rock," even though the murder weapon had not been made public; they claimed that only the murderer could know that a rock was used as the murder weapon.

In the days before DNA was used in criminal trials, the eyewitness identifications and Bloodsworth's own statements were good enough for a conviction. Bloodsworth appealed, saying that the police had put a rock on the table in the interrogation room, evidently trying to make him feel guilty. His "terrible" mistake had been not buying his wife the taco salad that he had promised her. Although Bloodsworth won a new trial, the second jury convicted him again, but he did not receive the death penalty at his second trial.

Advances in technology, particularly PCR, which allows testing for minute amounts of DNA, gave Bloodsworth new hope. In 1992, his attorney persuaded prosecutors to release evidence in the case—including the victim's clothing and underwear, a stick found near the body, and samples taken from the autopsy—for an independent lab to perform DNA testing on the items. After the lab concluded that semen stains taken from the evidence did not match Bloodsworth's blood sample, the FBI conducted its own tests, with the same results. Bloodsworth had spent nine years behind bars, guilty only of failure to deliver a taco salad. Ironically, it was DNA testing that allowed police to finally identify another suspect. The DNA taken from the crime scene matched that of another man, who was arrested on unrelated attempted rape and murder charges just weeks after Bloodsworth was arrested.

Unfortunately, Kirk Bloodsworth is not alone in having been convicted of a crime that he did not commit. However, his case led the way to helping some of the many others who share his predicament. He was the first person convicted of a capital offense to be exonerated by a DNA test, but there have been others. Testifying before Congress in 2003, attorney Peter Neufeld told a House committee that at least 132 Americans had been exonerated by post-conviction DNA testing, after serving a total of 1,397 years in prison, and that 12 of them had been on death row.[63]

> • **Is there an acceptable error rate for convictions?**

Neufeld and fellow attorney Barry Scheck founded the Innocence Project at a New York law school to help the many people in prisons and on death row following an erroneous conviction. Aided by volunteer attorneys and law students, this and similar innocence programs around the country help to use DNA evidence to overturn wrongful convictions. Despite their best efforts, however, they simply do not have the resources necessary to help everyone who might need it—such appeals can take many hours of legal and scientific research and years of winding through the court system. Advocates of post-conviction DNA exoneration believe that many people should have their cases reexamined—a process that could lead to the real perpetrators being caught, but due to state laws and lack of funding, the help is not forthcoming.

Police and prosecutorial misconduct often leads to wrongful convictions.

The American system of criminal justice is supposed to protect the rights of the accused. A person charged with a crime is presumed innocent until proven guilty by a court of law. The Bill of Rights provides many specific protections, both from investigation and prosecution. For example, people cannot be searched or arrested without grounds for suspicion, and people have the right to have an attorney when being interrogated. At trial, the accused have additional rights, such as the right not to testify against oneself, and the right to cross-examine witnesses. Even with all of these protections and the many others extended by legislatures and courts throughout the years, people are convicted of crimes that they did not commit, as evidenced by the Kirk Bloodsworth case.

How does this happen? In some cases, novelist and attorney Scott Turow believes, police and prosecutors distort the facts and cover up evidence of innocence. He gives the example of the rape and murder of a young girl in 1982, which the press called "The Case That Broke Chicago's Heart." With the community outraged and an election looming, the state's attorney promised justice, and two men were convicted of the crime. Turow became involved with the appeal of one of the men, Alejandro Hernandez, against whom charges were finally dropped in 1995. In one of his trials, a police expert had testified that shoe prints that were "about a size 6" were found at the crime scene; the prosecution was trying to link the prints to the diminutive Hernandez, who wore a size 7 shoe. As it turned out, the prosecutor made no effort to clarify that the prints were a size 6 girl's shoe, not a size 6 man's shoe that conceivably could have been worn by Hernandez. Worse yet, another man confessed to the rape and murder, as well as another very similar crime, in 1985, but the prosecutors continued to pursue Hernandez and his codefendant for another ten years. Eventually, however, DNA tests confirmed the other man's confession.

- **What should be done to police and prosecutors who put an innocent person in prison?**

Turow testified to Congress that such behavior by police and prosecutors is more likely in crimes, such as sexual assaults and murders of children, that cause widespread anger in the community. He stated:

> The highly emotional nature of these cases can also occasionally become the by-way to overreaching by prosecutors or police. Such overreaching occurred in many of the thirteen exonerated cases [in Illinois], but those cases

remain a small subset of capital prosecutions. In my experience, the overwhelming majority of prosecutors and law-enforcement officers seek to be fair. But special challenges are presented by highly visible cases, especially ones where an outraged community demands results and where the thought of someone perceived as a vicious criminal going free is nigh on to intolerance to those whose job it is to safeguard the public. The high rate of reversals in capital prosecutions—about 65% in Illinois, which is in line with national figures derived in a recent study—is due to a number of factors, but one I venture to say, after reading

THE LETTER OF THE LAW

DNA Backlog Elimination Act of 2000

(a) Findings.—Congress finds that—

(4)   DNA testing was not widely available in cases tried prior to 1994;

(5)   new forensic DNA testing procedures have made it possible to get results from minute samples that could not previously be tested, and to obtain more informative and accurate results than earlier forms of forensic DNA testing could produce, resulting in some cases of convicted inmates being exonerated by new DNA tests after earlier tests had failed to produce definitive results;

(6)   DNA testing can and has resulted in the post-conviction exoneration of more than 75 innocent men and women, including some under sentence of death;

(7)   in more than a dozen cases, post-conviction DNA testing that has exonerated an innocent person has also enhanced public safety by providing evidence that led to the apprehension of the actual perpetrator;

(8)   experience has shown that it is not unduly burdensome to make DNA testing available to inmates in appropriate cases;

hundreds of such opinions, is the frequency with which prosecutors and law-enforcement officers feel obliged to push the envelope.[64]

Post-conviction DNA testing helps to identify the real perpetrator of crimes.

The case cited by Turow is not the only instance in which reexamining DNA evidence has led not only to the exoneration of people who had been erroneously convicted, but also to the identification of the real criminal. Peter Neufeld of

(9) under current Federal and State law, it is difficult to obtain post-conviction DNA testing because of time limits on introducing newly discovered evidence; ...

(11) only a few States have adopted post-conviction DNA testing procedures;

(12) States have received millions of dollars in DNA-related grants, and more funding is needed to improve State forensic facilities and to reduce the nationwide backlog of DNA samples from convicted offenders and crime scenes that need to be tested or retested using upgraded methods;

(13) States that accept such financial assistance should not deny the promise of truth and justice for both sides of our adversarial system that DNA testing offers. ...

(b) Sense of Congress.—It is the sense of Congress that—

(1) Congress should condition forensic science-related grants to a State or State forensic facility on the State's agreement to ensure post-conviction DNA testing in appropriate cases. ...

Source: DNA Backlog Elimination Act of 2000, Pub. L. No. 106-561 (2000).

the Innocence Project told a House committee in 2003 that, in at least thirty-four cases, the same evidence that helped to exonerate someone convicted of a crime also helped to identify the actual perpetrator.[65] Sometimes the evidence might have even been sitting right under the prosecutor's nose. In the Hernandez case described by Turow, another man had already confessed, and his DNA matched. In other cases, the connection might not be so obvious; therefore, the Innocence Project's model statute allows judges to order the DNA profiles from the crime scene evidence entered into a DNA database so that it can be compared to the profiles in the database.

Post-conviction testing can also be helpful in cases in which the trial left unanswered questions. Former New York City prosecutor Harlan Levy, in his 1996 book *And the Blood Cried Out*, discusses the infamous "Central Park Jogger" case, in which a twenty–seven-year-old investment banker was raped and left for dead while jogging in Central Park. On the night of the attack, a group of about forty teenagers had gone "wilding"—randomly attacking victims—in Central Park. The crimes played to public hysteria because the teenagers were minorities while most of their victims were white, and because the crimes had no apparent motive or plan.

Five teens confessed to raping and beating the jogger, but when the DNA test from the rape kit came back, the results did not match any of the five defendants. This left prosecutors in an awkward position, wrote Levy. The prosecutors decided not to attack the reliability of the test results, because DNA testing had so much promise for prosecutors. "We . . . started from the premise that we did have the right guys. . . . So we had to figure out what had gone wrong here, why the DNA results had turned out the way they did."[66]

The prosecution suggested that the five teens had participated in the rape and beating, but another unknown person was the rapist, and therefore the five teens' DNA was not found. Another suggestion was that the victim's emergency medical treatment had delayed the gathering of rape evidence, and therefore some of the DNA evidence was destroyed.

In 2002, another man confessed to being the rapist and claims to have acted alone. (The victim had no recollection of the attack and did not know how many people attacked her.) A DNA test confirmed that he was the rapist. In a cruel bit of irony, that man was Matias Reyes, whom Levy had profiled in his book's introductory chapter. Reyes was one of the first people that New York prosecutors had "brought down" using DNA evidence, and Levy noted, "At the time Reyes was sentenced in 1991, the new genetic evidence that had played a crucial role in sending him to prison for life was just gaining wide acceptance."[67]

Unfortunately, DNA technology had not yet progressed to the point that police or prosecutors could use a database to compare the DNA from the Central Park rape to the string of rapes for which Reyes was prosecuted. The five people convicted, however, had for years claimed that police had coerced their confessions, and had the justice system reexamined the seemingly controversial verdict earlier, the DNA database might have implicated Reyes earlier. After Reyes' confession was confirmed, a judge vacated the guilty verdicts of the five men convicted in the case, although a panel assembled by the New York Police Department found reason to doubt that Reyes had indeed acted alone and to believe that the men had participated in the attack, as prosecutors had originally claimed.

State laws do not offer people a meaningful opportunity to challenge convictions.

The DNA Backlog Elimination Act of 2000 offered money to the states to eliminate their backlogs in processing crime scene evidence and in processing convicted offender profiles for data banking, on the condition that the states agreed "to ensure post-conviction DNA testing in appropriate cases."[68] Some advocates, however, believe that the states have not done

Gary Dotson's Exoneration

On the evening of July 9, 1977, the complainant was walking home from work when two men [allegedly] forced her into the back seat of a car and raped her. She also testified that one of the men tried to write words on her stomach using a broken beer bottle. She was then pushed from the car onto the street.

In July 1979 Gary Dotson was convicted of aggravated kidnapping and rape. He was sentenced to not less than 25 and not more than 50 years .... The prosecution's case included ... [evidence that] Dotson was identified by the victim from a police lineup....

In March 1985 the victim recanted her testimony. She said she had fabricated the rape to hide a legitimate sexual encounter with her boyfriend.... At the hearing on Dotson's motion for a new trial, the same judge from the original trial refused to order a new trial. His reasoning was that the complainant was more believable in her original testimony than in her recantation. . . . The governor [of Illinois] stated that he did not believe the victim's recantation and refused to pardon Dotson. On May 12, 1985, however, the governor commuted Dotson's sentence to the 6 years he had already served, pending good behavior. . . . [After] Dotson was arrested in a barroom fight, and his parole was revoked. In 1988 Dotson's new attorney had DNA tests conducted that were not available at the time of the alleged rape....

The lab performed PCR DQ alpha tests that showed that the semen on the victim's undergarments could not have come from Dotson but could have come from the victim's boyfriend....

Dotson's conviction was overturned on August 14, 1989, after he had served a total of 8 years.

Source: National Institute of Justice, *Convicted by Juries, Exonerated by Science: Case Studies in the Use of DNA Evidence to Establish Innocence After Trials* (Washington: U.S. Department of Justice, 1996).

enough to ensure meaningful access to DNA testing for people convicted of crimes. Urging the Senate to enact more effective measures to ensure that states provide opportunities for post-conviction testing, Barry Scheck gave the following illustration of why such laws are needed:

> [A] law student from the Kentucky Innocence Project located evidence from a bloodstain near a broken window that investigators believed came from the assailant in an old murder case. The bloodstain has never been tested and the inmate, Michael Elliott, who is serving a life sentence, claims it will prove him innocent and identify the real offender. Instead of consenting to tests, the local prosecutor moved in the trial court to destroy the evidence—and the motion was granted! An appeal to a Kentucky Court of Appeals was successful in preventing the destruction order from issuing, . . . but, due in part to the fact that Kentucky's post-conviction DNA statute only covers inmates on death row, not inmates serving life terms, Michael Elliott has not been able to obtain [in] Kentucky courts an order mandating that the evidence be preserved and a DNA test conducted.
>
> Instead, we have had to file a . . . civil rights lawsuit in federal court seeking access to the evidence for purposes of post-conviction DNA testing, based on . . . constitutional theories. . . . [69]

The Innocence Project has produced a "Model Statute for Obtaining Post-conviction DNA Testing,"[70] which it would like to see each of the states adopt. Among its provisions are:

- People convicted of a criminal offense have the right to petition for retesting of evidence, including people who have already finished serving time and people who pleaded guilty.

- People have the right to legal representation
  if DNA evidence is material to the appeal.

- Investigators must retain all biological evidence
  for the duration of a person's sentence, including any time the person must register as a
  sex offender.

- The state must pay for post-conviction
  DNA testing.

- **Who should make the decision whether an appeal is likely to
  be meritorious or frivolous?**

Another obstacle in providing post-conviction DNA
testing has been a lack of funding for DNA testing, both for
exoneration of convicted offenders and investigation of
unsolved crimes. The Innocence Project has also been a key
member of a coalition pushing for federal funding of post-
conviction DNA testing for the purpose of exoneration. One
of the several versions of the Advancing Justice Through
DNA Technology Act under deliberation in Congress in 2004
includes the Innocence Protection Act. In addition to guar-
anteeing people convicted of federal offenses the protections
of the Innocence Project's model statute, the Innocence
Protection Act would establish the Kirk Bloodsworth Post-
Conviction DNA Testing Grant Program. This program sets
aside $5 million per year for several years to allow states to
do post-conviction testing.[71]

Summary

Civil libertarians and defense attorneys have created quite a
stir by exposing a number of wrongful convictions using

DNA testing. Too often, however, people are denied the right to post-conviction DNA testing, either by state law, a judge's decision, or lack of resources. Advocates would like to see that every person convicted of a crime have the right to have biological evidence, if any, retested in order to challenge the validity of the conviction. Too often, erroneous convictions have resulted from police and prosecutorial misconduct.

The Most Pressing Use for DNA Evidence Is Solving Cold Cases

E ach time a person is exonerated of a crime for which a jury has returned a guilty verdict, critics say that the incident reveals a fundamental flaw in the justice system. Victims' rights advocates, however, point to a different type of flaw. Hundreds of thousands of crimes remain unsolved, their perpetrators walking free, while their victims are either dead or living in constant fear. Although it might be true that more than one hundred people have been exonerated by retesting DNA evidence, these cases represent a miniscule percentage of criminal convictions, the vast majority of which are sound. More telling, prosecutors and victims' rights groups say, is the staggering numbers of crimes for which crime scene evidence has not been tested for DNA. In testimony to Congress in July 2003, Sarah Hart of the National Institute of Justice estimated that crime scene evidence had not been processed in hundreds of thousands of cases. Additionally, she said, between 200,000 and 300,000 DNA samples had been collected from convicted offenders but not yet tested for placement in automated databases. Furthermore, an estimated 500,000 to 1 million convicted offenders had not yet provided samples as required by law.[72]

Hart testified as to the enormous investigatory power that DNA holds, if only the crime scene evidence and offender profiles could all be processed. Congress had acted before, in 2000, to provide funding for reducing the backlog of crime scene and convicted offender DNA testing, and while helpful, much work remained to be done. In fact, detectives had to stop investigating many unsolved crimes when there were no more leads to go on, referring to these crimes as "cold cases."

Hart told members of Congress a story that showed that if DNA testing is done, no case is "too cold" to solve:

> In 1977, a six-year-old girl disappeared while vacationing with her family in Reno, Nevada. Her remains were found two months later. DNA testing was not available in 1977, and the case remained unsolved for twenty-three years. In 2000, renewed investigative efforts resulted in a DNA test of the victim's clothing and entry of the resulting DNA profile into the Nevada State DNA database. A database search revealed a match to a man who had been on parole since 1976 for a previous sexual assault of a minor. The man pled guilty to the murder in October 2000.[73]

Although recognizing the value of exonerating people who are truly innocent of the crimes for which they have been convicted, any situation involving scarce resources involves choices. With hundreds of thousands of cases that could be reviewed, either to locate an unknown offender, or to reconfirm the conclusion reached by a jury, most prosecutors and victims' rights advocates would like to see the lion's share of whatever money is available spent on solving cold cases, rather than reopening the cases of people already convicted at trial.

Hearing frivolous appeals renews victims' trauma.

The impact of post-conviction DNA testing is not limited to the convicted offenders who take the tests; the victims of the crimes are also part of the equation. When a St. Louis woman was raped in 1985 at the age of fifty-nine, it was an incredibly traumatizing experience. Nearly two decades later, she had to relive that trauma when investigators came to gather information about the rape. The convicted rapist had requested DNA testing, and to complete the test, investigators had to rule out other sources of

Prosecutors' Group Urges Devoting Resources to Cold Cases

Advances in DNA technology hold enormous potential to enhance our quality of justice even more dramatically. However, significant increases in resources are needed to enlarge forensic laboratory capacity and expand DNA databases. No other investment in our criminal justice system will do more to protect the innocent, convict the guilty and reduce human suffering.

In keeping with these beliefs, the National District Attorneys Association has supported funding for forensic laboratories to eliminate backlogs in the testing of biological samples from convicted offenders and crime scenes. Funding by the federal government is a critical component in realizing the full potential of DNA testing. Federal funding should not be contingent upon a state's adoption of any specific federally mandated and unfunded legislation such as post conviction relief standards....

[The] absence of a biological sample, in and of itself, is not necessarily dispositive of innocence. There can be many reasons why an identifiable biological sample was not available at a crime scene, yet an individual can still be guilty of the commission of a crime. In many cases DNA testing results that exclude an individual as the donor of biological evidence do not exonerate a suspect as innocent. In a sexual assault involving multiple perpetrators, for

DNA found at the crime scene. They took a DNA sample from the woman using a buccal swab, and, more disturbingly, inquired about her sex life at the time. After all of this anguish, the crime scene DNA was conclusively linked to the convicted rapist. The woman, however, was so traumatized by the whole affair that she did not even want to hear the results. The woman, who is deaf and reads lips, refused to look when her son tried to tell her.

- **Could anything be done to evaluate a case before exposing the victim to renewed testing and questioning?**

Hart told Congress that incidents like this necessitate restrictions on post-conviction DNA testing. While groups such

example, a defendant may have participated in the rape without depositing identified DNA evidence. In such cases, the absence of a sample or a comparative exclusion is not synonymous with exoneration. Moreover, as powerful as DNA evidence is, it tells us nothing about issues such as consent, self-defense or the criminal intent of the perpetrator. . . . Post-conviction testing should be employed only in those cases where a result favorable to the defendant establishes proof of the defendant's actual innocence, exonerating the defendant as the perpetrator or accomplice to the crime. . . . Requiring only that the results of a DNA test produce material, non-cumulative evidence, and not specifically prove innocence, allows defendants to waste valuable resources, unnecessarily burden the courts and further frustrate victims. Decisions about such issues as the categories of convicted persons to be offered post-conviction relief and the standards to be employed are best made at the state or local level, where decisions can reflect the needs, resources and concerns of states and communities.

The resources for DNA testing are finite. Conducting frivolous or non-conclusive tests could mean that another test freeing an innocent person or apprehending a guilty person would not be done in a timely manner or at all.

Source: Senate Committee on the Judiciary, *Protecting the Innocent: Proposals to Reform the Death Penalty.* 107th Cong, 2d Sess. (2002) (testimony of Paul A. Logli).

as the Innocence Project would like to see everyone convicted of a crime have the right to request DNA testing, other people believe that testing should only be available in cases in which a wrongful conviction seems likely. Hart testified:

> [Although] post-conviction DNA testing is necessary to correct erroneous convictions imposed prior to the ready availability of DNA technology, experience also points to the need to ensure that post-conviction DNA testing is appropriately designed so as to benefit actually innocent persons, rather than actually guilty criminals who wish to game the system or retaliate against the victims of their crimes. Frequently, the results of post-conviction DNA testing sought by prisoners confirm guilt, rather than establish innocence. In such cases, justice system resources are squandered and the system has been misused to inflict further harm on the crime victim.[74]

The absence of DNA evidence does not prove actual innocence.

In cases such as the St. Louis rape, in which DNA testing merely reconfirms the conviction, at least it can be argued that closure is even more certain for the victims. In other cases, however, closure is not so easily obtainable. In a significant percentage of cases, the crime scene evidence has been misplaced or destroyed, and in others, there was no biological evidence collected. Most troubling of all are the cases in which DNA evidence does not match the person convicted of the crime, but there remains reason to believe that the person was nonetheless involved in the crime in some way.

- **Should prosecutors be allowed to argue a different theory of the crime—such as that the person convicted was an accomplice—or should they be required to prove the details of the crime beyond a reasonable doubt?**

Each time groups such as the Innocence Project help to free someone from prison, newspaper headlines carry stories of the grave injustice inflicted upon the released prisoners. However, some law enforcement officials doubt that the "exonerations" always tell the whole story. Many crimes are committed in which no biological evidence is found, and many people are convicted without DNA evidence. In crimes committed by more than one person, each is guilty of the crime. In a rape, if one person holds the victim while another rapes her, both are guilty of rape. Many people believe therefore that when post-conviction DNA testing reveals another person's DNA was present at the crime scene, this finding does not necessarily exonerate the convicted offender from participation in the crime.

In 2003, the *Winston-Salem Journal* ran a series of in-depth articles reexamining the conviction of Darryl Hunt for raping and murdering a woman in 1984, a case that has fanned the flames of racial tension because the victim was white and Hunt is African American. The series strongly implies that Hunt was wrongly convicted, and he was released from prison on Christmas Eve of 2003. Critics had alleged racism was the cause of Hunt's continued imprisonment: A 1994 DNA test of the rape kit did not match Hunt's DNA, but Hunt had remained in prison. Prosecutors continued to maintain Hunt's guilt, however, saying he either was a participant or had committed the rape without leaving semen as evidence. District attorney Tom Keith remarked, "When we looked at it all, the DNA was not as significant as you think it is." [75] Although prosecutors eventually sided with Hunt, the victim's family continued to believe that he was involved.

Similar arguments have been made about the five men who confessed their involvement in the Central Park Jogger rape case, but whose convictions were vacated after DNA evidence linked the crime to another man, Matias Reyes, who claimed to have acted alone. A panel formed by the New York Police Department concluded: "The consistencies found in the defendants' statements, the informal remarks made by the defendants at various times, the corroborative testimony of other witnesses, the absence of a convincing motive for Reyes and suspicion of his general credibility, lead us to conclude that it is more likely than not that the defendants participated in an attack upon the jogger."[76]

Conservative columnist Ann Coulter was more blunt in her assessment of the role of the five men whose convictions were ultimately vacated. In her *townhall.com* column, she wrote: "Liberals so long to claim that every criminal is innocent, they forget that . . . it was well-known at the time that the semen found on the jogger did not match any of the defendants. . . . The five primitives on trial were described as among those who attacked the jogger. No new evidence contradicts the five guilty verdicts."[77]

Solving cold cases brings closure to victims and prevents future crimes.

Although proponents of post-conviction DNA testing list identifying the true perpetrator as one of the benefits, such cases are few and far between. Although post-conviction testing advocates can point to several dozen cases in which post-conviction testing has identified another culprit, such cases are very rare in the grand scheme of DNA testing. By the end of 2002, Virginia alone had identified more than one thousand culprits using its DNA database. However, Virginia's "hit" rate skyrocketed only after the state devoted a great deal of money to processing crime scene evidence and entering the DNA profiles of convicted offenders and arrestees into its database.

The director of Virginia's crime lab system, Paul Ferrara, testified before Congress that additional federal funding for reducing backlogs could prevent needless tragedies, stating, "The only long-term solution to backlogs of crime scene evidence is to fund the education, training and employment of the estimated 5,000 to 10,000 new forensic scientists that will be needed in the coming years to meet this growing demand."[78] He told the tragic story of a man who was released from jail on a shoplifting charge in early 1999, while Virginia was experiencing a large backlog of cases. Although police suspected the man of a prior rape, and the state had his DNA sample and crime scene evidence, the backlog in cases had prevented the lab from testing either sample, and prosecutors could not charge him in the rape. Eleven days after he was released from jail, he raped and murdered another woman.

In addition to preventing tragedies like the one described by Ferrara, law enforcement officials believe that solving cold cases can also offer peace of mind to crime victims and their families. Assistant U.S. Attorney General Mary Lou Leary recounted the story of a woman whose rape was solved by a determined detective:

> This is the story of Kelly. At the time that Kelly was raped Florida was not processing nonsuspect cases because they didn't have the funding to do so, but three years later there was one detective who was persistent, and he asked that they dust off the rape kit from Kelly's case. . . .
>
> When they entered that data into Florida's local DNA database, they found almost instantly a match with the FBI's CODIS system. . . . [The rapist's profile matched that of a] man who was already serving a 25-year sentence for beating and raping a woman just six weeks before Kelly's attack.[79]

Even though the perpetrator was already in prison, said Leary, solving such crimes "can mean hope for victims who are lost in a kind of a purgatory of not knowing who or where their attackers might be and whether they might come back and attack them again."[80] Additionally, because many rapists are eventually released from prison, linking unsolved cases to people already serving time can help to ensure that they spend more time in prison.

DNA evidence is conclusive enough to allow trial of very old cases.

In criminal law, a statute of limitations sets limits on the amount of time during which someone can be charged with a criminal offense. Typically, time limits vary with the seriousness of the crime, with murder often having no statute of limitations. As explained by Sarah Hart of the National Institute of Justice:

Rape Survivor Finds Peace Because of DNA "Cold Hit"

There is no way for you to understand how what is done in the DNA labs can mean the difference between life and death without taking you back to March 3, 1989.... [when] a masked stranger forcibly took me out of my home where he blindfolded, robbed and repeatedly raped me. The sound of his voice rang through my ears as a deafening clamor, "remember, I know where you live and I will come back and kill you if you tell anyone." As soon as I was set free, I ran upstairs to my sleeping husband, waking him with the words, "he got me Rob, he got me." I begged him not to call the police, I pleaded with him because I feared this man would keep his promise to return and kill me. But the police officer in my husband knew that we couldn't let this go unreported. He also convinced me of the importance of going to the hospital, for he knew we may need the evidence collected with the rape kit. All I wanted to do was to take a shower and wash it all away.

There was no escaping the pain, no escaping the fear.... It was always there. It was there in my waking hours as well as in my dreams. On many occasions, my husband would be awakened in the middle of the night to the sound of blood curdling screams from the nightmares. It was at this point that I began to realize that I could not and would not live this way. Death seemed to be the only alternative, the only answer that would end this horrible nightmare that had become my life.... I didn't know relief from my pain sat on a shelf, just waiting for the manpower and funds to test my attacker's DNA sample and place it in the data bank....

A statute of limitations usually reflects a legislative judgment that the burden of prosecuting an old crime may outweigh its benefits. It balances the need to prosecute serious crimes with concerns that a delayed prosecution may be unreliable given the passage of time and faded memories. A statute of limitations may also encourage law enforcement officials to investigate promptly suspected criminal activity.[81]

As George Li sat at his computer in the Virginia Division of Forensic Science on July 24, 1995, on what probably seemed to him to be just another day at the lab, he had no way of knowing what effect his work that day would have on my life and those around me. On this day Mr. Li entered a prisoner's blood sample into the computer and it automatically began its cross check against previously entered samples.... Not only had they identified my rapist but he was already in prison for another crime ... and he was put there 6 months after I was attacked. Finally they had unpacked the box that contained my release from fear ... my freedom had been delivered.

For the first time in six and a half years, I could feel myself breathe. I felt validated. There was a real name and a real face to go with the nightmare. Everyone would know that I was telling the truth, that it was real. Finally, I could quit looking over my shoulder. No longer did I have to drive around in circles hoping a neighbor would drive by so I could get the courage to get out of my car to go into my own front door if no one else was home. Unfamiliar noises no longer left me panic-stricken. I no longer scanned faces in a crowd to see if he was following me. Suicide was no longer a consideration. And finally, my husband is grateful that I don't wake him up anymore in the middle of the night with the ear-piercing screams. Within myself, the healing had begun and peace had come at last. Because of your efforts this man is off the streets for good. The jury gave Norman Jimmerson 2 life sentences plus 25 years with no chance of parole.

Source: Senate Judiciary Committee, *Justice for Sexual Assault Victims: Using DNA Evidence to Combat Crime*, 107th Cong, 2d Sess. (2002) (testimony of Debbie Smith).

• **Do statutes of limitations make sense given the conclusiveness of DNA evidence? How can a person challenge the validity of the testing?**

In the past, most states did have a statute of limitations for rape cases, despite the serious nature of the offense. Rape cases, however, are the most likely to produce DNA evidence, which can be a very conclusive indicator of guilt, and several states have eliminated the statute of limitations in rape cases. In arguing for elimination of statutes of limitations in federal crimes, Hart explained to Congress:

> The dependability of DNA evidence does not diminish over time and it produces reliable verdicts years after the crime was committed. [The] mechanical application of a fixed statute of limitations can bar a trial even where law enforcement officials have promptly investigated the crime and sought to use DNA evidence. For these reasons, we have recommended that the provisions governing the time period for commencing prosecution in Federal cases be amended so as to toll the limitation period for prosecution in felony cases in which the perpetrator is identified through DNA testing. This reform is necessary to realize the full value of the DNA technology in solving crimes and protecting the public from rapists, killers, and other serious offenders.

The DNA identification system solves crimes by collecting DNA samples from offenders and matching the resulting DNA profiles to DNA found in crime scene evidence. However, this process proves to be futile where the sample taken from an offender matches, for example, rape kit DNA from a rape committed some years previously, but prosecution is impossible because it is time-barred. For example, in Federal law, the limitation period for the prosecution of most offenses is five years. . . . So if a person who commits a rape avoids identification for five years, he has quite likely acquired permanent immunity from prosecution—even if DNA matching conclusively identifies him as the perpetrator five years and one day after the commission of the crime. Rape cases involving DNA matches which occur after the expiration of a restrictive statute of limitations have already been seen in the current operation of the DNA identification system, and their number will increase as the DNA databases grow and the use of the DNA technology expands.[82]

Summary

Law enforcement officials and victims' rights advocates believe that if scarce resources are to be dedicated to DNA testing, the emphasis should be on unsolved crimes, rather than on cases already ruled upon by a jury. While agreeing that post-conviction testing is useful in some cases, in other cases where the results are not doubtful, reopening the case can re-traumatize the victim needlessly, and the results of DNA tests are not always reliable indicators of innocence. On the other hand, solving cold cases can offer victims closure and prevent future crimes. Increasingly, jurisdictions are eliminating the statute of limitations in rape cases, because DNA is a reliable enough indicator of guilt that no case is "too cold."

CONCLUSION

The Future of
DNA Evidence

Many experts believe that DNA technology will continue to develop, making testing faster, more accurate, and more conclusive. As technology improves, police will collect DNA evidence in an increasing number of investigations, and it might even become the first lead that investigators follow. The Research and Development Working Group of the National Institute of Justice predicts that by the year 2010,

> [p]ortable, miniaturized instrumentation . . . will provide analysis at the crime scene with computer-linked remote analysis. This should permit rapid identification and, in particular, quick elimination of innocent suspects.
>
> By this time, there should be a number of markers available that identify physical traits of the individual

contributing the DNA. It should be possible, using this information, to narrow the search for a suspect, with consequent increases in the accuracy and efficiency of operation.[83]

> • **Should police be allowed to predict a suspect's appearance based on a blood droplet? Will that lead to more racial profiling by police?**

While the benefits to law enforcement of a pocket DNA tester that can provide clues to a suspect's appearance are obvious, such technology is certain to raise objections from civil libertarians, and perhaps as the technology becomes more intrusive, of large segments of the population. Are we ready for a day when police start rounding up everyone with red curly hair simply because some evidence at a crime scene suggests that a rapist has red curly hair?

Changes are bound to take place outside of the laboratory as well, as the police and the courts adapt their ways to reflect the growing use of DNA technology. Criminals will also change their ways, just as the advent of fingerprinting forced them to use gloves. Courts and legislators undoubtedly will struggle with the question of when the use of DNA technology simply goes too far and begins to threaten everyone's freedom. Already, the use of DNA technology in the criminal justice system leaves many unanswered questions.

Will courts require DNA evidence for prosecution?

Many victims' rights advocates have hailed the use of DNA evidence to solve and prosecute rape cases because it so often provides conclusive evidence of guilt. DNA evidence, however, could prove to be a double-edged sword to prosecutors, who are likely to find that seemingly solid cases are being challenged on a lack of DNA evidence, even though other evidence pointed to the defendants. Attorney Jim Wooley warned law enforcment officials that they would be facing a "DNA expectation," which he explained as follows:

> [Judges and juries,] nudged along by able, informed defense attorneys[,] will be expecting that DNA will be done increasingly and in cases involving evidence you never thought would involve DNA, you know, envelope flaps, stamps, cigarette butts, shirt cuffs, shirt collars, telephone mouthpieces, rims of drinking glasses.
>
> If it's not done in cases, I think fact finders are going to ask you why. They're going to ask and they're going to put this to you: *Why didn't you process the crime scene and handle the evidence in a way that maximizes the chance that we could have done some DNA testing?*[84]

• How should the court system deal with allegations of planted DNA evidence?

A related question is whether the availability of DNA evidence in many rape and sexual assault cases will increase the difficulty of obtaining convictions in cases in which DNA evidence is not available. In a significant majority of rape and sexual assault cases, the victim knows the attacker, and therefore DNA evidence would not be needed to establish the identity of the attacker. Some people involved in combating domestic violence worry that because in many instances rape victims who know their attackers do not get a rape exam—and therefore no DNA evidence is collected—prosecutors will become less likely to prosecute such cases, and juries will become less likely to convict. Several groups have spoken out against focusing police efforts on "unknown attacker" cases, maintaining that any rape or sexual assault is a serious crime that should be prosecuted to the fullest extent of the law.

Will criminals find ways to beat DNA collection procedures?

A growing concern among law enforcement officials is that criminals will find ways of preventing police from recovering DNA evidence. Criminals can avoid eyewitness identification by wearing a mask, and they can avoid leaving fingerprints by wearing gloves. Some criminals already take steps to prevent leaving DNA evidence at a crime scene. For example, some rapists have worn condoms to avoid leaving semen as evidence, while other rapists have forced their victims to bathe after the attack, in the hope of destroying evidence. (This tactic is not a very effective means of avoiding detection.) Similarly, criminals could seek to clean any blood they left behind if injured in the attack. Other steps to avoid detection could be as simple as not spitting or discarding cigarette butts at the crime scene.

Some criminals have taken some elaborate steps to try to foil prosecutors' use of DNA evidence. One convicted rapist claimed that he had been wrongly convicted, and that he just happened to share the same DNA profile as the real rapist. While he was in prison, an accomplice smuggled out some of the rapist's semen, and then staged a rape. When the police processed the rape kit, they discovered that it matched the convicted rapist's profile, even though he was in prison at the time of the alleged rape. He had called attention to himself, however, by suggesting to police that they investigate the rape, and they quickly got to the bottom of the plot. This stunt, however, raises the question of whether criminals will start leaving "dummy DNA" at a crime scene to confuse investigators.

The seemingly indisputable nature of DNA evidence raises the very real concern that framing someone for a crime is now very easy. Many people thought that the alleged framing in the O. J. Simpson murder case—with police planting drops of the victims' blood in Simpson's home and car, and planting Simpson's blood on crime scene evidence—was an unlikely scenario. Framing someone for a murder, however, could be as easy as planting one of his or her cigarette butts at the scene of the crime. The ease with which such a frame-up can occur raises the possibility that courts will be flooded with such defenses.

What will the Supreme Court say about DNA data banking?

Although a number of federal courts have issued rulings concerning the widespread collection of DNA profiles, and most courts have approved such laws, the Supreme Court has not yet had the occasion to issue a ruling on the issue. Although the relatively conservative, pro-law enforcement court is likely to uphold collecting DNA samples from convicts, the question of collecting DNA from arrestees is less clear. Murkier still is the issue of whether police can ask everyone in a community for a DNA sample, and then use a person's reluctance as justification for seeking a search warrant compelling a saliva sample. Even some of the Court's conservative members are concerned with issues of privacy. For example, Justice Anthony Kennedy wrote the majority opinion in a case ruling that laws forbidding sodomy are unconstitutional, using language that reflects a concern that the government should not intrude on the most private aspects of its citizens' lives. While not related to DNA testing, a person's genetic makeup is one of the most private aspects of his or her being, and Kennedy's opinion reflects a renewed concern for privacy in today's world:

> Liberty protects the person from unwarranted government intrusions into a dwelling or other private places. In our tradition the State is not omnipresent in the home. And there are other spheres of our lives and existence, outside the home, where the State should not be a dominant presence. Freedom

extends beyond spatial bounds. Liberty presumes an autonomy of self that includes freedom of thought, belief, expression, and certain intimate conduct.[85]

Summary

As DNA technology expands, both police and criminals will find new ways of dealing with its apparent conclusiveness. As law enforcement officials seek to collect DNA samples from more and more people, the U.S. Supreme Court might have concerns about protecting the privacy of everyday citizens.

NOTES ///////

1. Research and Development Working Group, National Institute of Justice, *The Future of Forensic DNA Testing* (Washington, D.C.: U.S. Department of Justice, 2000), p.18.

2. Ibid., p. 17.

3. Ibid., p. 19.

4. National Institute of Justice, *National Law Enforcement Summit on DNA Technology* (July 27–28, 2000), part 6. Transcript available online at *http://www.ojp.doj.gov/nij/dnasummit/trans-6.html*.

5. Laurence D. Mueller, "The DNA Typing Controversy and NRC II," in *Statistics in Genetics* (New York: Springer-Verlag, 1999).

6. *60 Minutes II*, "DNA Testing: Foolproof?" (May 28, 2003) Transcript available online at *http://www.cbsnews.com/stories/2003/05/27/60II/printable555723.shtml*.

7. *Vermont* v. *Pfenning*, No. 57–4–96 (Dist. Ct. Vt., April 6, 2000).

8. U.S. Constitutional Amend. 6.

9. National Institute of Justice, National Law Enforcement Summit, part 6.

10. Ibid., part 8.

11. Henry C. Lee and Frank Tirnady, *Blood Evidence: How DNA Is Revolutionizing the Way We Solve Crimes* (Cambridge, Mass.: Perseus, 2003), p. ix.

12. Research and Development Working Group, p. 24.

13. House Subcommittee on Crime, Terrorism, and Homeland Security, *Advancing Justice Through the Use of DNA Technology*, 108th Congress, 1st Session (2003) (Testimony of Peter J. Neufeld).

14. National Institute of Justice, *Convicted by Juries, Exonerated by Science: Case Studies in the Use of DNA Evidence to Establish Innocence After Trials* (Washington, D.C.: U.S. Department of Justice, 1996), p. xxi.

15. Michael C. Dorf, "How Reliable Is Eyewitness Testimony?" *Findlaw's Writ* (May 16, 2001). Available online at *http://writ.findlaw.com/dorf/20010516.html*.

16. House Subcommittee on Crime, Terrorism, and Homeland Security, *Advancing Justice*.

17. Vincent Bugliosi, *Outrage: The Five Reasons Why O. J. Simpson Got Away With Murder* (New York: W.W. Norton & Co., 1996), p. 139.

18. National Institute of Justice, *Convicted by Juries, Exonerated by Science: Case Studies in the Use of DNA Evidence to Establish Innocence After Trials*, p. xxii.

19. Ryan McDonald, "Juries and Crime Labs: Correcting the Weak Links in the DNA Chain," *American Journal of Law and Medicine* (Summer–Fall 1998).

20. U.S. Constitutional Amendment 4.

21. National Institute of Justice, National Law Enforcement Summit, part 1.

22. *U.S.* v. *Kincade*, No. 02–50380 (9th Circuit, October 2, 2003).

23. Ibid.

24. National Commission on the Future of DNA Evidence, National Institute of Justice, *Testimony of Barry Steinhardt, Associate Director, American Civil Liberties Union* (March 1, 1999).

25. National Institute of Justice, *National Law Enforcement Summit*, part 7.

26. Troy Duster, *Backdoor to Eugenics*, 2d. ed. (New York: Routledge, 2003), p.160.

27. Mark Rothestein, "Genetic Secrets: A Policy Framework," in *Genetic Secrets: Protecting Privacy and Confidentiality in the Genetic Era* (New Haven, Conn.: Yale University Press, 1997), p. 480.

28. Dorothy Nelkin and Lori Andrews, "DNA Identification and Surveillance Creep," in *Sociological Perspectives on the New Genetics* (London: Blackwell, 1999), p. 204.

29. Duster, p.159.

30. National Institute of Justice, National Law Enforcement Summit, part 1.

31. Ibid.

32. Rudolph W. Giuliani, 2000 State of the City address, January 13, 2000. Transcript available online at *http://www.nyc.gov/html/2000a/stcitytext2000.html.*

33. *U.S. v. Kincade,* No. 02–50380.

34. National Institute of Justice, National Law Enforcement Summit, part 7.

35. Ben Quarmby, "The Case for National DNA Identification Cards," *Duke Law & Technology Review* 2 (2003).

36. National Institute of Justice, National Law Enforcement Summit, part 7.

37. Ibid., part 2.

38. Ibid., part 7.

39. National Commission on the Future of DNA Evidence, *Testimony of Barry Steinhardt.*

40. *Weeks v. U.S.,* 232 U.S. 383 (1914).

41. *City of Indianapolis v. Edmond,* 531 U.S. 32 (2000).

42. *U.S. v. Kincade,* No. 02–50380.

43. Ibid.

44. *NewsHour with Jim Lehrer,* "Strands of Justice" (July 10, 1998). Transcript available online at *http://www.pbs.org/newshour/bb/law/july-dec98/dna_7-10.html.*

45. Christine Rosen, "Liberty, Privacy, and DNA Databases," *The New Atlantis* (Spring 2003).

46. National Commission on the Future of DNA Evidence, *Testimony of Barry Steinhardt.*

47. Stephen Braun, "Virginia Aggressively Uses DNA to Solve Other Cases," *Los Angeles Times* (January 13, 2003), A11.

48. National Commission on the Future of DNA Evidence, National Institute of Justice, *Racial Profiling* (July 10, 2000). Transcript available online at *http://www.ojp.doj.gov/nij/dnamtgtrans10/trans-11.html.*

49. House Subcommittee on Crime, Terrorism, and Homeland Security, *Advancing Justice Through the Use of DNA Technology.*

50. *Gaines v. Nevada,* 998 P.2d 166 (Nevada 2000).

51. National Institute of Justice, National Law Enforcement Summit, part 2.

52. Ibid., part 7.

53. Senate Committee on the Judiciary, *Department of Justice Oversight: Funding Forensic Sciences—"DNA and Beyond,"* 108th Congress, 1st Session (2003) (Testimony of Sarah v. Hart).

54. National Institute of Justice, National Law Enforcement Summit, part 2.

55. Ibid.

56. Ibid.

57. Ibid.

58. Ibid.

59. Richard Willing, "White House Seeks to Expand DNA Database," *USA Today* (April 15, 2003).

60. Giuliani, 2000 State of the City address.

61. Ibid.

62. Michael E. Smith, David H. Kaye, and Edward J. Imwinkelried, Editorial, "DNA Data From Everyone Would Fight Crime, Racism," *USA Today* (July 25, 2001).

63. House Subcommittee on Crime, Terrorism, and Homeland Security, *Advancing Justice Through the Use of DNA Technology.*

64. Senate Committee on the Judiciary, *Reducing the Risk of Executing the Innocent: Report on the Illinois Governor's Commission on Capital Punishment,* 107th Congress, 2d Session (2002) (Testimony of Scott Turow).

65. House Subcommittee on Crime, Terrorism, and Homeland Security, *Advancing Justice Through the Use of DNA Technology.*

66. Harlan Levy, *And the Blood Cried Out: A Prosecutor's Spellbinding Account of the Power of DNA* (New York: Basic Books, 1996), p. 79.

67. Ibid., p. 16.

68. DNA Backlog Elimination Act of 2000, Public Law No. 106–651 (2000).

69. Senate Judiciary Committee, *Protecting the Innocent: Proposals to Reform the Death Penalty*, 107th Congress, 2d Session (2002) (Testimony of Barry Scheck).

70. See *http://www.innocenceproject.org/docs/Model_Statute.html*.

71. H.R. 3214, 108th Congress §3 (2003).

72. Senate Committee on the Judiciary, *Department of Justice Oversight*.

73. Ibid.

74. Ibid.

75. Phoebe Zerwick, "State: DNA Results Irrelevant," *Winston-Salem (N.C.) Journal* (November 22, 2003). Part of special series, "Murder, Race, Justice: The State vs. Darryl Hunt," available online at *http://darrylhunt.journalnow.com*.

76. New York Police Department, *Central Park Jogger Case Panel Report* (January 27, 2003).

77. Ann Coulter, "New York Times Goes Wilding on Central Park Jogger," *townhall.com* (October 17, 2002). Available online at *http://www.townhall.com/columnists/anncoulter/ac20021017.shtml*.

78. House Subcommittee on Crime, Terrorism, and Homeland Security, *Advancing Justice Through the Use of DNA Technology* (Testimony of Paul B. Ferrara).

79. National Institute of Justice, National Law Enforcement Summit, part 7.

80. Ibid.

81. Senate Committee on the Judiciary, *Department of Justice Oversight*.

82. Ibid.

83. Research and Development Working Group, pp. 3–4.

84. National Institute of Justice, National Law Enforcement Summit, part 7.

85. *Lawrence v. Texas*, No. 02–101 (June 26, 2003).

Books

Bugliosi, Vincent. *Outrage: The Five Reasons Why O. J. Simpson Got Away With Murder.* New York: W.W. Norton & Co., 1996.

Conrad, Peter, and Jonathan Gabe, eds. *Sociological Perspectives on the New Genetics.* London: Blackwell, 1999.

Duster, Troy. *Backdoor to Eugenics,* 2d. ed. New York: Routledge, 2003.

Lee, Henry C., and Frank Tirnady. *Blood Evidence: How DNA Is Revolutionizing the Way We Solve Crimes.* Cambridge, Mass.: Perseus, 2003.

Levy, Harlan. *And the Blood Cried Out: A Prosecutor's Spellbinding Account of the Power of DNA.* New York: Basic Books, 1996.

National Institute of Justice. *Convicted by Juries, Exonerated by Science: Case Studies in the Use of DNA Evidence to Establish Innocence After Trials.* Washington: U.S. Department of Justice, 1996.

Research and Development Working Group, National Commission on the Future of DNA Evidence, National Institute of Justice. *The Future of Forensic DNA Testing.* Washington: U.S. Department of Justice, 2000.

Rothstein, Mark, ed. *Genetic Secrets: Protecting Privacy and Confidentiality in the Genetic Era.* New Haven: Yale University Press, 1997.

Websites

American Civil Liberties Union
www.aclu.org
National organization, with state affiliates, concerned with civil liberty issues, including the rights of the accused. Information about the privacy aspects of collecting DNA samples.

Campaign for Criminal Justice Reform
www.cjreform.org
Organization dedicated to preventing and overturning wrongful convictions and addressing flaws in the justice system. Advocates post-conviction DNA testing.

Denver District Attorney
www.denverda.org
Prosecutes crimes in Denver, Colorado. Links to court cases and laws regarding the admissibility of DNA evidence.

Electronic Privacy Information Center
www.epic.org
Research and advocacy center concerned with privacy implications of technology. In-depth description of DNA privacy issues.

The Innocence Project
www.innocenceproject.org
Provides legal representation regarding post-conviction DNA testing to people wrongfully convicted of crimes. Information about funding and access to post-conviction DNA testing.

National Association of Criminal Defense Lawyers
www.nacdl.org
National organization offering information about using DNA in criminal defense and post-conviction appeals.

National District Attorneys Association
www.ndaa.org
National organization representing prosecutors. Information about using DNA in prosecution and related policy issues.

National Institute for Justice
www.ojp.usdoj.gov/nij/
Responsible for federal research and development of crime-fighting tools. Sponsors the National Commission on the Future of DNA Evidence, which offers many online publications.

National Organization for Women
www.now.org
Prominent national organization active in many women's issues. Information about using DNA evidence to solve and prevent rapes.

Refuse & Resist
www.refuseandresist.org
Organization opposing "police state measures." Editorials about DNA data-bank issues.

Scientific Testimony: An Online Journal
www.scientific.org
Journal seeking to expose and discuss flaws in the way scientific testimony is presented in court. Information about possible weaknesses in DNA evidence and related testimony.

Virginia Department of Criminal Justice Services
www.dcjs.org/forensic/
Considered a leader in using DNA data banks to apprehend criminal suspects. Extensive information about DNA data banks and their impact on law enforcement.

Cases and Statutes

California v. *Kocak*, No. SCD110465 (Super. Ct. Cal. 1995)
During trial, prosecution witness revealed that report implicating defendant had confused the defendant's DNA profile with the victim's profile, thus mistakenly implicating the defendant.

Watts v. *State*, 733 So.2d 214 (Miss. 1999)
State Supreme Court ruled that unsubstantiated allegations of contamination could not cast reasonable doubt on defendant's conviction.

Gaines v. *Nevada*, 998 P.2d 166 (Nev. 2000)
State Supreme Court upheld collection of DNA sample from convicted burglar.

City of Indianpolis v. *Edmond*, 531 U.S. 32 (2000)
U.S. Supreme Court held that individualized suspicion is required for searches with primary purose of law enforcment.

DNA Backlog Elimination Act of 2000, Pub. L. No. 106-561 (2000)
Provides funding to states to eliminate backlog of crime scene evidence and convicted offender DNA profiles. Encourages but does not require access to DNA testing for convicted offenders.

Vermont v. *Pfenning*, No. 57-4-96 (Dist. Ct. Vt., 6 April 2000)
Trial court rejected the introduction of the results of a new type of DNA testing that had not been widely studied.

U.S. v. *Kincade*, No. 02-50380 (9th Cir., 2 Oct. 2003)
Federal appeals court ruled that collection of DNA samples from convicted offenders, without individualized suspicion, violates the Fourth Amendment.

Green v. *Berge*, No. 01-4080 (7th Cir., 9 Jan. 2004)
Rejecting the reasoning of the *Kincade* case, another federal appeals court rules that collection of DNA from convicted offenders does not require individualized suspicion.

Concepts and Standards

Actual innocence
Bodily intrusion
Buccal swab
Cold case
Cold hit
Contamination of evidence
DNA
DNA data banks
DNA dragnet
DNA profiles

Exoneration
Expectation of privacy
Individualized suspicion
Junk DNA
PCR
Post-conviction DNA testing
Recidivism rates
RFLP
Statute of limitations
STR

117

Beginning Legal Research

The goal of POINT/COUNTERPOINT is not only to provide the reader with an introduction to a controversial issue affecting society, but also to encourage the reader to explore the issue more fully. This appendix, then, is meant to serve as a guide to the reader in researching the current state of the law as well as exploring some of the public-policy arguments as to why existing laws should be changed or new laws are needed.

Like many types of research, legal research has become much faster and more accessible with the invention of the Internet. This appendix discusses some of the best starting points, but of course "surfing the Net" will uncover endless additional sources of information—some more reliable than others. Some important sources of law are not yet available on the Internet, but these can generally be found at the larger public and university libraries. Librarians usually are happy to point patrons in the right direction.

The most important source of law in the United States is the Constitution. Originally enacted in 1787, the Constitution outlines the structure of our federal government and sets limits on the types of laws that the federal government and state governments can pass. Through the centuries, a number of amendments have been added to or changed in the Constitution, most notably the first ten amendments, known collectively as the Bill of Rights, which guarantee important civil liberties. Each state also has its own constitution, many of which are similar to the U.S. Constitution. It is important to be familiar with the U.S. Constitution because so many of our laws are affected by its requirements. State constitutions often provide protections of individual rights that are even stronger than those set forth in the U.S. Constitution.

Within the guidelines of the U.S. Constitution, Congress—both the House of Representatives and the Senate—passes bills that are either vetoed or signed into law by the President. After the passage of the law, it becomes part of the United States Code, which is the official compilation of federal laws. The state legislatures use a similar process, in which bills become law when signed by the state's governor. Each state has its own official set of laws, some of which are published by the state and some of which are published by commercial publishers. The U.S. Code and the state codes are an important source of legal research; generally, legislators make efforts to make the language of the law as clear as possible.

However, reading the text of a federal or state law generally provides only part of the picture. In the American system of government, after the

118

legislature passes laws and the executive (U.S. President or state governor) signs them, it is up to the judicial branch of the government, the court system, to interpret the laws and decide whether they violate any provision of the Constitution. At the state level, each state's supreme court has the ultimate authority in determining what a law means and whether or not it violates the state constitution. However, the federal courts—headed by the U.S. Supreme Court—can review state laws and court decisions to determine whether they violate federal laws or the U.S. Constitution. For example, a state court may find that a particular criminal law is valid under the state's constitution, but a federal court may then review the state court's decision and determine that the law is invalid under the U.S. Constitution.

It is important, then, to read court decisions when doing legal research. The Constitution uses language that is intentionally very general—for example, prohibiting "unreasonable searches and seizures" by the police—and court cases often provide more guidance. For example, the U.S. Supreme Court's 2001 decision in *Kyllo* v. *United States* held that scanning the outside of a person's house using a heat sensor to determine whether the person is growing marijuana is unreasonable—*if* it is done without a search warrant secured from a judge. Supreme Court decisions provide the most definitive explanation of the law of the land, and it is therefore important to include these in research. Often, when the Supreme Court has not decided a case on a particular issue, a decision by a federal appeals court or a state supreme court can provide guidance; but just as laws and constitutions can vary from state to state, so can federal courts be split on a particular interpretation of federal law or the U.S. Constitution. For example, federal appeals courts in Louisiana and California may reach opposite conclusions in similar cases.

Lawyers and courts refer to statutes and court decisions through a formal system of citations. Use of these citations reveals which court made the decision (or which legislature passed the statute) and when and enables the reader to locate the statute or court case quickly in a law library. For example, the legendary Supreme Court case *Brown* v. *Board of Education* has the legal citation 347 U.S. 483 (1954). At a law library, this 1954 decision can be found on page 483 of volume 347 of the U.S. Reports, the official collection of the Supreme Court's decisions. Citations can also be helpful in locating court cases on the Internet.

Understanding the current state of the law leads only to a partial under-standing of the issues covered by the POINT/COUNTERPOINT series. For a fuller understanding of the issues, it is necessary to look at public-policy arguments that the current state of the law is not adequately addressing the issue. Many groups lobby for new legislation or changes to existing legislation; the National Rifle Association (NRA), for example, lobbies Congress and the state legislatures constantly to make existing gun control laws less restrictive and not to pass additional laws. The NRA and other groups dedicated to various causes might also intervene in pending court cases: a group such as Planned Parenthood might file a brief *amicus curiae* (as "a friend of the court")—called an "amicus brief"—in a lawsuit that could affect abortion rights. Interest groups also use the media to influence public opinion, issuing press releases and frequently appearing in interviews on news programs and talk shows. The books in POINT/COUNTERPOINT list some of the interest groups that are active in the issue at hand, but in each case there are countless other groups working at the local, state, and national levels. It is important to read everything with a critical eye, for sometimes interest groups present information in a way that can be read only to their advantage. The informed reader must always look for bias.

Finding sources of legal information on the Internet is relatively simple thanks to "portal" sites such as FindLaw (*www.findlaw.com*), which provides access to a variety of constitutions, statutes, court opinions, law review articles, news articles, and other resources—including all Supreme Court decisions issued since 1893. Other useful sources of information include the U.S. Government Printing Office (*www.gpo.gov*), which contains a complete copy of the U.S. Code, and the Library of Congress's THOMAS system (*thomas.loc.gov*), which offers access to bills pending before Congress as well as recently passed laws. Of course, the Internet changes every second of every day, so it is best to do some independent searching. Most cases, studies, and opinions that are cited or referred to in public debate can be found online—and *everything* can be found in one library or another.

The Internet can provide a basic understanding of most important legal issues, but not all sources can be found there. To find some documents it is necessary to visit the law library of a university or a public law library; some cities have public law libraries, and many library systems keep legal documents at the main branch. On the following page are some common citation forms.

//////////

COMMON CITATION FORMS

Source of Law	Sample Citation	Notes
U.S. Supreme Court	*Employment Division v. Smith*, 485 U.S. 660 (1988)	The U.S. Reports is the official record of Supreme Court decisions. There is also an unofficial Supreme Court ("S. Ct.") reporter.
U.S. Court of Appeals	*United States v. Lambert*, 695 F.2d 536 (11th Cir.1983)	Appellate cases appear in the Federal Reporter, designated by "F." The 11th Circuit has jurisdiction in Alabama, Florida, and Georgia.
U.S. District Court	*Carillon Importers, Ltd. v. Frank Pesce Group, Inc.*, 913 F.Supp. 1559 (S.D.Fla.1996)	Federal trial-level decisions are reported in the Federal Supplement ("F. Supp."). Some states have multiple federal districts; this case originated in the Southern District of Florida.
U.S. Code	Thomas Jefferson Commemoration Commission Act, 36 U.S.C., §149 (2002)	Sometimes the popular names of legislation—names with which the public may be familiar—are included with the U.S. Code citation.
State Supreme Court	*Sterling v. Cupp*, 290 Ore. 611, 614, 625 P.2d 123, 126 (1981)	The Oregon Supreme Court decision is reported in both the state's reporter and the Pacific regional reporter.
State Statute	Pennsylvania Abortion Control Act of 1982, 18 Pa. Cons. Stat. 3203-3220 (1990)	States use many different citation formats for their statutes.

page:
12: AP Graphics
53: © Morocco Flowers/Index Stock Imagery
60: Associated Press, AP/Joerg Sarbach

Cover: © SIU/Visuals Unlimited

ALAN MARZILLI, of Durham, North Carolina, is an independent consultant working on several ongoing projects for state and federal government agencies and nonprofit organizations. He has spoken about mental health issues in more than twenty states, the District of Columbia, and Puerto Rico; his work includes training mental health administrators, nonprofit management and staff, and people with mental illness and their family members on a wide variety of topics, including effective advocacy, community-based mental health services, and housing. He has written several handbooks and training curricula that are used nationally. He managed statewide and national mental health advocacy programs and worked for several public interest lobbying organizations in Washington, D.C., while studying law at Georgetown University.